What The Critics Are Saying About
THE VIETNAM ECCLESIASTES

I'm in the pig motel poem. Life is a curled tail, Berry, and don't forget it.
-Oinky Pink

Many last stanzas snappy in Yeats's music-box sense. - Swep

I wear sunglasses 24-7. - Weep Eye

I like animals with tongues, and there are many here. - Blow Zoo

Why no mention of Blanche, the dope-smoking mama cat? - Leonard

The Berry I knew seemed normal. - Rudy Burl

Many of these poems require a professor to understand. Like having your mother with you in the whore house. - Hoof and Mouf Disease

Berry, as a gynoastrology student, couldn't find the star on a woman's bosom. - Dr. Bobo

What a puppy yelp. - Sgt. Death

All of these short, like Berry in his sag thing. - Emily Dickinson

A writer is an eraser, but Berry chewed both ends. - Walter Whitman

Berry should listen to the preacher of Ecclesiastes. 'Of making many books there is no end; and much study is a weariness of the flesh.' - Preacher

Vietnam Ecclesiastes

1945-1975

D.C. Berry

Illustrations by Dan Drew

Copyright © 2007 by D.C. Berry
Illustrations Copyright © 2007 by Dan Drew
All rights reserved.
First edition.

Illustrations: Dan Drew
Design: Sarah Crevelling and Colleen Marie Ryor

ISBN 0-9768993-1-0

Black Lawrence Press
Black River, New York

TABLE OF CONTENTS

ADVERTISEMENT: DON'T BE ON THE WRONG SIDE, YOU 15
To famous men, all the earth is a sepulcher. - Thucydides.

TRUMPET BLASTS JAPLAND 16
The first qualification of a soldier is fortitude under fatigue and privation. Courage is only the second; hardship, poverty and want are the best school for a soldier. - Napoleon.

GRASSHOPPER HO CHI AND PEACOCK PIERRE 17
Jugurtha was so crafty...that one never knew which was the more deadly — his presence or his absences. - Sallust.

FRANCE MUST HIT THE ROAD PRETTY DARN SOON 18
I renew my request that our Air Force mechanics be withdrawn from Indo-China....Soon we may have to fight or run. - Stennis.

DIEN BIEN FASHION d'OBJECT 19
*It is not merely cruelty that leads men to love war, it is excitement. - Beecher.
There are empty fields now where Troy once was. - Ovid.*

GENERAL DUNG'S VICTORY PARADE 20
You can't stop me. I spend thirty thousand men a month. - Napoleon.

PIERRE SURRENDERS FRENCH KISS, 1954 21
Using United States ground forces in the Indo-China jungle would be like trying to cover an elephant with a handkerchief—you just can't do it. - Knowland.

VIET MINH COLD BOYS 22
Even if he has nothing to eat a warrior should still pick his teeth. - Japanese proverb.

PREMIER DIEM AH SO ME SAY SO 23
Even to command a flock of sheep is pleasant. - Spanish proverb.

TWO-TAIL TUX MAN 24
First I engage, then I see what can be done. - Napoleon.

POLE THE GOLF 25
In every combat the eyes are the first part subdued. - Tacitus.

MOI DEALS WITH IT 26
The young soldier should have a lively eye...waist small, his build compact, his legs and feet... a little height may be dispensed with. - Flavius Vegetius Renatus.

ROULETTE d'HOUDINI NAM 27
The poisoned arrow was the Stone Age equivalent of a nuclear deterrent....The slow action of the poison left a stricken adversary ample time in which to avenge the suffering that lay ahead of him. - Warneburg.

GENERAL PAUL D. HARKINS TECHNICOLORS ANTEATER MOVIE 28

TUG OF WAR HANDS AND EYES   29
I have never talked or corresponded with a person knowledgeable in Indochinese affairs who did not agree that had elections been held as of the time of the fighting, possibly 80 percent of the population would have voted for the Communist Ho Chi Minh as their leader. - Eisenhower.

HOT MONK AND COOL DOG   30
How many seeming impossibilities have been accomplished by men whose only resource was death. - Napoleon.

DI ANN MARKET DALMATIAN   31

RICE MAN AND WATER BO GO TECHNO   32

MADAME NHU PLAYS HERSELF   33
An ally has to be watched just like an enemy. - Trotsky.

FLAG VEX   34

BUDDHA TOURIST AGENCY   35
The Lacedaemonians have temples dedicated not only to Fear, but to Death, and Laughter, and the like. They honour Fear, not as a malevolent divinity to be shunned, but because they think that the constitutions of states are mainly upheld by Fear. - Plutarch.

EXAM FOR TANK KIDS   36

THROW NGUYEN'S ASS OUT ON THE DANCE FLOOR   37

GULF OF HONKY TONKIN   38
The United States got into the guerrilla war in South Vietnam by mistake because Yo-Yo [Secretary of Defense Robert S. McNamara] went there and told these boys to start shooting when we were only supposed to be instructing. - Goldwater.

MOTHER EARTH MESSES WITH FATHER TIME   39
God shall see to it that war shall always recur, as a drastic remedy for ailing humanity. - Treitschke.

DADA NAM   40
War is a singular art. I assure you that I have fought sixty battles, and I learned nothing but what I knew when I fought the first one. - Napoleon.

THE ROMANCE OF THE CLEAN MARINES   41
Gentlemen: The enemy stands behind his entrenchments armed to the teeth. We must attack him and win, or else perish. Nobody must think of getting through in any other way. If you don't like this you may resign and go home. - Frederick the Great.

WHITE NIGHTGOWN FLOWER ARIA FOR MEN   42
War is the child of pride, and pride the daughter of riches. - Swift.

SERGEANT DEATH GOLFS BOB   43

PIGGYVILLE PORKS AWHILE   44
We must never forget that if the war in Vietnam is lost...the right of free speech will be extinguished throughout the world. - Nixon.

AMBUSH MOVIE: SURPRIxE, JOHN FONDA 45
The more we Americanize the war...the more we make the war unwinable. - Schlesinger.

THE JUMPIN JACK FLASH PADDY 46

FOG DOGGIE STYLE 47

NORTH VIETNAM TURNAROUND 48

GRENADE HAMLET CALAMITY 49
Grenadoes are small shells, concave Globes or hollow Balls, some made of Iron, some of Tin, others of Wood, and even of Pasteboard; but most commonly of Iron, because the splinters of it do most execution....These are thrown by hand into places where Men stand. - Anonymous.

FLIES SING COPPERTONE 50

PHANTOM JET SKY DOODLES 51

GREENERY d'NAM 52

MEKONG LUCIFER COOL 53
Nationalism is an infantile disease. - Einstein.

HOSPITAL VAMPIRETORIUM 54

SKI VIETNAM TODAY OR TOMORROW 55
War is like love, it always finds a way. - Brecht.

LINES OUT THE BOO HINEY 56
All the tall men with mustaches are placed in the first rank....Men who have mustaches, but who are less good-looking, are placed in the second rank....The shortest men go to the third rank, and the tallest men without mustaches to the fourth. - Prussian drill-book.

BEER JESUS 57

LOVERBOY ROSES BY HOWITZER 58
To give ground, provided they rally again, is considered rather as a prudent stratagem, than cowardice. They carry off their slain even while the battle remains undecided. The greatest disgrace that can befall them is to have abandoned their shields. A person branded with this ignominy is not permitted to join in their religious rites.
- Tacitus.

FNG THE VANILLA GRRR 59
I am more afraid of our mistakes than our enemies' designs. - Pericles.

NUMBNUTS CONSIDERS BAYONET 60
There is no weapon too short for a brave man. - Steele.
A bayonet is a weapon with a worker at each end. - Socialist slogan.
A weapon is an enemy even to its owner. - Turkish proverb.

ONION MOUTH SPEAKS WAR FACE 61

TRENCHES AND PETTICOAT COMBAT 62

AGENT ORANGE, ORANGE CRUSH, NO PROB 63

POETS COMMIT HIGH BARD   64
He looked back to Caesar, and said: General, I will act in such a manner today, that you will feel grateful to me, living or dead. - Caesar.

PRIVATE HOLLYWOOD VEGAS   65

TIMEX PUGILISTES   66

ADMIRAL BEETLE TELLS GENERAL BEETLE   67

THE GUARD REPORTS SEEING THE LIGHT   68
In this new kind of war, new methods of managing it were invented...our men were taught by experience to light their fires in one place, and keep guard in another. - Caesar.

JOKER REPORTS UNPLEASANTNESS OVERCOME   69
You can't say civilization don't advance, however, for in every war they kill you a new way. - Rogers.

THE VIETNAM PIN-UP CALENDAR   70

B-52 BOMB CREEP   71
If you hide yourselves, they shall fire your houses without mercy, hang up your bodies wherever they find them, and scare your ghosts. - The Governor of Worcester.

BUNKER CAT QUICKEES   72

THE SNIPER SOUVENIRS GI   73

PECKER NOSE CUSTOMIZE   74

VALENTINE'S DIRTY DAY   75

NGUYEN FREAKS HITCHCOCK   76

TET MAN A MESS   77
Many victories have been and will be suicidal to the victors. - Plato.

SLEEP LUCKY VIA HOT DAMN   78

TUNNEL RAT FROGMAN   79

NGUYEN'S FRIGHTENING OUCH   80

THE KITE GRENADE VOCALIZES NGUYEN   81
Who shows mercy to an enemy, denies it to himself. - Bacon.

CAR BOMB TONY   82
I begin to regard the death and mangling of a couple of thousand men as a small affair, a kind of morning dash. - Sherman.

CAR BOMB JITTERBUG   83
You will usually find that the enemy has three courses open to him, and of these he will adopt the fourth. - Moltke.

CAM RANH BAY HARD-ON   84

BOOM TOWN TROUT   85
War is a game in which princes seldom win, the people never. - Colton.

TAIL CAPITALISM AND MARX FOK U 86
RELIGION GETS THE JOB DONE AGAIN 87
The only war I ever approved of was the Trojan war; it was fought over a woman and the men knew what they were fighting for. - Phelps.

CURVE THE ORIENT 88
Fighting is a contest between man and man more than between brain and brain. - Fuller.

THE GENERAL'S POTTY ISN'T A HONKY TONK 89
The General is the Minister of Death, and cannot be responsible to the heavens above, to the earth below, to the enemy in front, or to the emperor in his rear. - Tu Mu.

THE BAND AND THE TALL BOY 90
The Lacedaemonians moved slowly and to the music of many flute-players. - Thucydides.

THE LIPSTICK WAR GEOMETRY 91
RAT MAN THE CAT MAN RAT 92
When a man goes into the army, he presently changes, not only his dress, but his behavior, his company, his air, his manner of speaking, and affects to throw off all appearance of any thing that may look like common life and conversation. For a man that is to be ready equipped for any kind of violence, despises the formal garb of a Citizen. - Machiavelli.

VIDALIA SLIM NGUYEN DELIVERS 93
It is fighting against a great disadvantage to fight against those who have nothing to lose. - Guicciardini.

PICASSO PEAK, OR DALI'S, NOT GAUGUIN'S (BECAUSE) 94
The Roman combination of the heavy javelin with the sword...produced similar results... to those attained in modern warfare by the introduction of bayonet muskets; the volley of javelins prepared the way for the sword encounter, exactly in the same way as a volley of musketry now precedes a charge with the bayonets. - Fuller.

THE PRICK 25 RADIO 95
Stout branches were cutdown and their ends stripped of their bark and sharpened to a point....There were five rows in each trench...and all who stepped in would impale themselves on the sharp stakes. The men called them grave-stones. - Caesar.

US EMBASSY WALL, OF ALL THINGS 96
We have dropped twelve tons of bombs for every square mile of North and South Vietnam. - R. Kennedy.

THE SAG IN YOUR COT IS PERSONAL 97
MY LAI AND THE SILVER PLATTER 98
A Cistercian monk, being asked how the Catholics were to be distinguished from heretics answered: Kill them all! God will know his own. - The Percy Anecdotes.

LUCK OF THE BUTT 99
Balls were playing across me: the sound of them is curious enough, as if it were composed of the humming of tops, the gurgling of water, and the whistling of birds. - Goethe.

NAPALM FLORAL DE BOOM   100
A single death is a tragedy. A million deaths are a statistic. - Stalin.

ARTY GOSH ALMIGHTY   101
Every gunner should know that it is good for him to drink, and eat a little meat, before he discharges any piece of artillery, otherwise the fumes of the saltpetre and brimstone may damage his brain. - Tartaglia.

NIEMAN MARCUS NGUYEN POWERGLIDE   102

THE PARIS PEACE TABLE SQUARES THE CIRCLE   103
North Vietnam cannot defeat or humiliate the United States. Only Americans can do that. - Nixon.

CATCHING BERNINI'S TROUT   104

PLATO MEETS MA BELL AND   105
The advantages are nearly all on the side of the guerrilla in that he is bound by no rules, tied by no transport, hampered by no drill-books, while the soldier is bound by many things, not the least by his expectation of a full meal every so many hours. - Wavell.

THE WATER BUFF'S MUSTACHE DRAWS HIGH COMMENT   106
The number of medals on an officer's breast varies in inverse proportion to the square of the distance of his duties from the front line. - Montague.

ALICE, THE AIR MATTRESS   107
I find I have liked all of the soldiers of different races who have fought with me and most of those who have fought against me. This is not strange, for there is a freemasonry among fighting soldiers that helps them to understand one another even if they are enemies. - Slim.

HAMBURGER HILL DONG THIS   108

PEACE BARBIE   109

KENT STATE CAMBODIA, DEAR MOM   110
Democracy is the best system of government yet devised, but it suffers from one great defect — it does not encourage those military virtues upon which, in an envious world, it must frequently depend for survival. - Du Maurier.

OO   111
Since both are slaves to desperation the art of war and the art of the courtesan are sisters. - Aretino.

THE EYE OF APRIL MAN   112
If a wound hath befallen you, a wound like it hath already befallen others: we alternate these days of successes and reverses among men, that God may know those who have believed, and that He may take martyrs from among you. - Mohammed.

THE MOHAWKS MOON SOME MOTHER'S SON   113
All the Britons, without exception, stain themselves with woad, which produces a bluish tint, and this gives them a wild look in battle. They wear their hair long and shave the whole of their body except the head and the upper lip. - Caesar.

DONUT DOLLY'S BOOBS 114
*I divide officers into four classes — the clever, the lazy,
the stupid, and the industrious. - Hammerstein.*

DIDDYBOPPING BUD POPPING 115
Movement is the safety-valve of fear. - Hart.

PRESIDENT NIXON SUCKY DOG 116
We are in a chamber-pot and we are going to be shat upon. - Ducrot.

COCKTAILS CELEBRATING VIETNAMIZATION 117
The wine is poured and we must drink it. - Marshal Ney.

WHITE HOUSE TOILET PAPER 118
*Happiness lies in conquering one's enemies, in driving them in front of oneself,
in taking their property, in savoring their despair, in outraging their wives and daughters.
- Genghis Khan.*

NAD KNOCKER NIGHT OWL 119
The sword often incited a man to fight. - Homer.

FRAG, THE MIDNIGHT SNIFF 120

THE FOREHEAD MAN 121

BEEHIVE CANNONBALLS HEAVY BLUES 122
*You should not have a favorite weapon. To become over familiar with one weapon
is as much a fault as not knowing it sufficiently well. - Musashi.*

NOISE TICK BLONG 123
*A much more horrible butchery took place in the city, where a weak and defenseless
crowd of women and children were massacred by their own people. - Livy.*

MOUTH A GO-GO 124

PEACE TALKS PARIS CAFE KITCHEN 125

CRAWDAD & THE SECRET PEACE TALKS 126
Force, and fraud, are in war the two cardinal virtues. - Hobbes.

INVASION DAPPER CHIC 127
The English conquered us; they are far from being our equals. - Napoleon.

CIGARETTE MOMENT 128
The wings of man's life are plumed with the feathers of death. - Drake.

SOLITARY CONFINEMENT ANTI-MATTER 129

THE NOT MUCH WEASEL CURSE 130

THE BOXED AERIALIST COMPUTES 131

PLUS RICE AND MINUS RICE 132

PROPOSAL FOR HUNCHBACK 133

TRAFFIC JAM AND RAM IT WHANG 134
Blood alone moves the wheels of history. - Mussolini.

BABEL 135
The guns and the bombs, the rockets and the warships,
are all symbols of human failure. - Johnson.

THE NUTRITIONAL HEED 136
In taking a state the conqueror must arrange to commit all his cruelties at once,
so as not to have to recur to them everyday. - Machiavelli.

THE BABY CRASH 137

CUCKOO KNEW IT 138
The quickest way of ending a war is to lose it. - Orwell.

FINE-PRINT HOLLYWOODS 139
And here is the lesson I learned in the Army. If you want to do a thing badly,
you have to work at it as though you wanted to do it well. - Ustinov.

MISS OLE MISS 140
The great nations have always acted like gangsters,
and the small nations like prostitutes. - Kubrick.

GONG SHOW NGUYEN, APRIL 1975 141
Thus the war terminated, and with it all remembrance of the veteran's service.
- Napier.

※ ※ ※

Quotations from THE DICTIONARY OF WAR QUOTATIONS,
ed. Justin Wintle, Free Press, 1989, and from QUOTATIONS VIETNAM:
1945-1970, ed. William G. Effros, Random House, 1970.

The following have been published or are forthcoming.

AURA ("The Water Buff's Mustache Draws High Comment," "Onion Mouth Speaks Warface"), BIRMINGHAM POETRY REVIEW ("FNG The Vanilla Grrr"), BLUE MESA REVIEW ("Car Bomb Jitterbug"), CONNECTICUT REVIEW ("Lines Out The Boo Hiney"), COOWEESCOOWEE ("Nieman Marcus Nguyen Powerglide"), EVANSVILLE REVIEW ("Mekong Lucifer Cool"), FLORIDA REVIEW (""), FRESHWATER ("Di An Market DALMATIAN"), GEORGETOWN REVIEW ("Ski Vietnan Today Or Tomorrow" and "Diddybopping And Bud Popping"), GEORGIA STATE REVIEW ("Sleep Lucky Via Ho Damn"), GETTYSBURG REVIEW ("Gulf Of Honky Tonkin" and "Madame Nhu Plays Herself"), GREEN MOUNTAINS REVIEW ("The Jumpin Jack Flash Paddy," "Fog Doggie Style," "North Vietnam Turnaround"), LAUREL REVIEW ("Rat Man the Cat Man Rat"),LITERARY REVIEW ("Grenade Hamlet Calamity," "Romance Of The Clean Marines), LUNA ("Crawdad And The Secret Peace Talks," "Peace Talks Paris Cafe Kitchen"), MAINSTREET RAG ("Alice, The Air Mattress"), MARGIE ("President Nixon Sucky Dog"), MASSACHUSETTS REVIEW ("Timex Pugilistes"), OHIO REVIEW ("Greenery d'Nam"), PHANTASMAGORIA ("Picasso Peak, Not Dali's, Not Gauguin's [Because]" "The Prick 25 Radio," "US Embassy Wall, Of All Things," "The Sag In Your Cot Is Personal," "My Lai And The Silver Platter"), PLEIADES ("Hospital Vampiretorium"), POETRY ("Cocktails Celebrating Vietnamization," "Frag, The Midnight Sniff"), REED MAGAZINE (General Paul D. Harkins Technicolors the Anteater Movie"), SALMAGUNDI ("Flies Sing Coppertone"), SALT FORK REVIEW (Pole The Golf") SATURDAY AFTERNOON ("Ambush Movie: SurpriXe, Jane Fonda" and "Gong Show Nguyen, April 1975"), SOUTH CAROLINA REVIEW ("Tet Man The Mess"), SOUTHEAST REVIEW ("Noise Tick Blong," "The Forehead Man," "Beehive Cannonball Heavy Blues," "Invasion Dapper Chic," "Peace Talks Paris Cafe Kitchen"), SOUTHERN POETRY REVIEW ("Phantom Jet Doodles"), TENNESSEE QUARTERLY ("Loverboy Roses By Howitzer" and "Mouth A Go-Go"), VERSE ("Trumpet Blasts Japland"), VIRGINIA QUARTERLY REVIEW ("Arty Gosh Almighty," "Catching Bernini's Trout"), WILLOW SPRINGS ("Tug Of War Hands And Eyes"), YALOBUSHA REVIEW ("Piggyville Porks Awhile" and "The Guard Reports On Seeing The Light").

※ ※ ※

Dedicated to Oinky Pink, Skinny Mama, Jamdanny Sham, Swep, Weep Eye, Blow Zoo, Leonard, Burnell, Rudy Burl, Chiller, Hoof & Mouf Disease, Crazy Mouth, Dr. Bobo Earl, Sgt. Death, Emily Dickinson, Walter Whitman, Preacher.

ADVERTISEMENT:
DON'T BE ON THE WRONG SIDE, YOU

(1945)

Is there any thing whereof it may be said, See, this is new?

Uncle Ho likes to advertise
BE RED COMRADE...OR DEAD
in life-size Vietnamese:

whacks off the head
of an old village gramps
too chummy with the round

eyes and then stakes this staring hat
on the gatepost. Heads are Uncle's
highnoon neon—tongue black,

eyes two white eggs, two blown fuses.
But silver fillings sparkle in the sun,
and blue flies buzz fluorescence.

TRUMPET BLASTS JAPLAND

(1945)

The thing that hath been, it is that which shall be.

Nguyen might not mash the lip
right honking kickass blare
on an old tincan French trumpet,

or mouth muffler, or whatever
he blows. Sounds like a moose
in puppy-love, underwater...

brown cheeks toad-puffed,
trumpet beneath a hairy lip
that resembles a burnt

French fry, Clark Gable neat, Nguyen toots
hot diggity, elbows high. He's run off
the Nips, spilled their sushi. Hep-cat

dog-howling Nguyen. In middle of
Roadrunner Road. Fleeing Nippons
leapfrog the wrecks and swim potholes.

Nguyen brays squawk jazz, some tune
about the hand grenades he flung
were hornet nests...jawbone

of Uncle Ho Chi Minh
cold-cocked legions, cross-bows
from fiddle strings. Forget accordions.

Nguyen owns the road.
no Lawrence Welk baton
need point which way to Tokyo.

Goodbye, all you Nippons.
Give Nguyen a magic horn,
and he thinks he's a moving van.

GRASSHOPPER HO CHI
AND PEACOCK PIERRE

    That which hath been is now.

Japs gone, France back: Uncle
Ho Chi's grasshopper veer,
versus Pierre's gymnastical

peacock. Game, hide-and-seek. Loser
can't lose. Uncle Ho hides,
and Pierre sneaks after

him and gets lost. Now, Pierre has
to stop. He squints around. He spies his peacock tail
and falls in love. The eyes

back there all ga-ga back. They roll
and flirt, and Pierre has himself
all to himself, alone in the jungle,

reaches his head around to his
hiney and gives
himself a long French kiss:

contorts a circle, makes
a hoop of himself, through which Ho
bounces through and escapes.

What is the game? Hide-and-seek, or
croquet romance, or hoop
Houdini's veer? Two points or three?

Just say which game, Uncle, and I'll be true,
You know I love me, but only
have eyes for you.

FRANCE MUST HIT THE ROAD
PRETTY DARN SOON

(1953)

Monsieur Pierre's problem is his shadow.
For one hundred years, Nguyen
had to wash and wax Pierre's shadow,

even his trains' shadows. Now Nguyen's
perched at the wheel, and poor Pierre's
shadow has shrunken smaller than

a bumper car—no cigs, no spare,
no brakes, even the poodles sniff
the end is near; and there's Pierre

not one single leg left
to pump the gas—scarecrow
that has swallowed his stick.

On sunny days, Pierre's shadow
shrinks down small as
a limo backfiring OH OH.

Black days it withers down small as
a roach—a roach de ville,
world's oldest hearse,

and shiniest—God's own polish—and all
six legs pumping the gas, racing
in smaller and smaller circles.

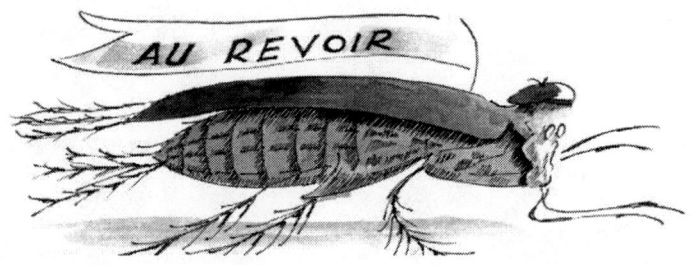

DIEN BIEN FASHION d'OBJECT

(May 1954)

**The wise have eyes in their head, but fools walk in darkness.
Yet I perceived that the same fate befalls all.**

Pierre's surrounded by the Nguyens.
One exit's left, a tree (climb to heaven), the limbs
stubby shot-offs. Looks like the skeleton

of a shark, a two-sided comb
twenty-feet tall, that frees
air-tangles knotted by napalm.

A hairdresser's trophy, this tree
of teeth. Or France's last backbone.
But what call it in Gay Paree?

A hat rack for pigeons,
a comb for traffic fumes.
Long Live Fashion.

GENERAL DUNG'S VICTORY PARADE

(July 1954)

The patient in spirit is better than the proud in spirit.

Dung's troops stand straight as fluorescent
tubes—you breaka, you buy—their hats
smushed-down lampshade rejects.

It's finis for Pierre and his greenback
buddies, their starched safari suits
and nuclear dingadoom threats.

Dung smiles like a ventriloquist.
Pouting French Legionnaire Germans salute,
fed-up with sour grapes and quiche.

The Nguyens step off, glide pitty-pat
like a long Christmas float,
a silent gazillion-thousand legged

caterpillar. No Nazi goose-step strut
for this viciously mild
people thing, whose head is General Dung,

whose tail is bumfuddle...
flows by in new Chinese sneakers,
so quiet their soles

sound like Twinkies,
these kickers of French ass,
and all size Small.

PIERRE SURRENDERS FRENCH KISS, 1954

Pierre putts his tank down
main-street Hanoi and crawls
out, clicks his heels at attention...

in white linen, medals
cut from a chimpanzee's
ass and turkey wattle.

Pierre is very lucky. He
must only kiss Ho's ax, not stretch
his neck. But when goes home, must leave

behind his French sauces and false
teeth and glass eyes
that are not blue. Can't take the French

kiss back, either. The French
kiss wasn't his in the first place.
Pierre stole the French kiss

straight from the Middle East.
That moaning python with twin tongues
slid directly off Noah's Ark.

And as for any kiss,
today's reconciliation—
nobody's kissing ass

today. But should Uncle Ho moon
Pierre, Pierre should at
least throw Uncle a courtesy wink.

VIET MINH COLD BOYS

No man can find out the work that God made.

Nguyen comes from that planet
near hell. Planet #7 Snowball—
coal chunks for eyes, steel sleet

for brains, and ice-cube testicles.
Snowman Nguyen, Nguyen Snowghost,
icicle penis melted by sunrise.

But sifts back silently at night.
Or did during the war. Now, Nguyen watches
France leave, stands squared-off at

robot attention: five-foot dick, buckles
sparkling, and sweating anti-freeze.
While Pierre boards the ship, Nguyen smiles

as if he invented ice cream,
French Vanilla, and Pierre can
taste how sweetful it is to win.

Too sweet, perhaps, as Nguyen's
teeth look soot gray
like a row of tiny tombstones.

PREMIER DIEM AH SO ME SAY SO

(1963)

He eyes his troops. Years back
he eyed New York City's mannequins—so
clean, plastic breath, the hairless sex.

But his men splash on buffalo
chemistry and gargle sardine
breathwarp. Diem walks the rows

like a penguin,
waddles in crotch
rot hell...sweats monk

juice, a Catholic
air-cooled hatless mystic,
the only limber dick

dressed in white French
silk suit
and undertaker's black

tie. His soldiers, Buddhists,
stare forward, planks
standing for Mary and Joseph.

After the inspection,
Diem puts the press to sleep,
preaches We winna, on and on.

Slicked-down wind-up evangelist.
Trundle
on off to bed, Diem's your night light—

his tongue your candle flame,
his jaw the moth that butts
the enemy senseless. Even the tall

Americans with their ski-slope
noses can't cool
down this buzzsaw spark plug.

If words are tools,
he's a monkey-wrench for parrots,
all mouth and no handle.

TWO-TAIL TUX MAN

(December 1961)

God hath made man upright; but they have sought out many inventions.

President Kennedy—King Croquet of Harvard,
Pulitzer Prize Pin-up, and Potentate
of Panties, Slip Ins, Slip Outs, and

Clip-on Bowtie Quickies—sure he could skulk
away from this Nam weenie roast,
fanned briskly by President Dwight D. Ike's

golf swing, but at the price of losing face.
And what's a tux without a mug? Or stroke
without the balls? Or rope without the noose

bow-tie? So, JFK sends in the troops,
thirty-three whirlybirds full of Combat
Kelly square-heads and just a little luck.

May be a risk to roll square-head dice, but
God pinned two tails on the elephant so it
wouldn't lose face, and that's worked-out.

POLE THE GOLF

We called him Pole
the Golf after we caught
him stroking his pickle

beneath the flag. Unlucky feet,
cueballs with no pocket, unlucky ears—
stepped on a mine, the sky went deaf.

The flagpole had been his Twiggy,
and just his luck—her blouse
when half lowered showed no titties.

MOI DEALS WITH IT

(1962)

The work of God, that a man cannot find out.

To both the North and South Vietnamese,
Mois aren't human. They're goons,
boonie bozo's, hillbilly trash.

But just like real humans,
these Mois
have humanoid problems,

such as this Moi's. Hanoi skinned his
father screaming, and Saigon tied his child
to a swinging gate for target practice.

This Moi is so human he plans to kill both sides.
Looks human, too: diaper around his hips
and one around his head, cut-outs for eyes—

like an Asian Bubba Earl, a Ku Klux
Klan freakoid, and every Vietnamese
he hammers proves he's human as

they were. More maybe, a Saint of Revenge
or St. What Do—he stands frozen,
an arrow in a world of melted compasses.

ROULETTE d'HOUDINI NAM

> Consider the work of God: for who can make that straight, which he hath made crooked.

Is Nguyen your Nguyen? His eyes Nguyen's eyes?
Which Nguyen's? You're drinking beer
with Nguyen at the Elvis

County Music Boy & Grill: this Nguyen your
Nguyen or Ho Chi's Congsta? Seems like
this Nguyen's your old VFW buster. But your

Nguyen might be Nguyen's twin at Dee Trot
Rockn Roll, next door. Which Nguyen's
your Nguyen? Same wide flip-flops, same black

shorts, same porcupine haircut, same Jack O'Lantern
teeth, but which one is your Carl
Perkins, and which Elvis? Which walked home in

blue suede highheels? Which Nguyen's Little
Richard, which one's Pat Boone? Don't blink
in Nam. Look back. Nam is a roulette wheel.

Which N's your N? Keep glancing back.
The one arrow you can't let stop
spinning is your shadow.

GENERAL PAUL D. HARKINS TECHNICOLORS ANTEATER MOVIE

(February 1962)

In this movie of dogass Nam, General
Paul's the director and most pretty pooch.
So many stars twinkle on his collar

you think poodle necklace
or Paul D's own Paul D Constellation. Paul D's
here to finish the French

flick ANTEATER, about sticking your snooze
in an ant bed (casting by Deja Vu)
and getting back your pecker tied in knots.

ANTEATER—not as a movie,
this time, forget Dum Dums and Coke,
this time for suppertime TV,

starring Paul D all lit up like
Liberace passing the beans,
soundtrack Pink Elephant...

the plan, out-French
the French,
eat ants alive.

TUG OF WAR HANDS AND EYES

Saigon's Catholic troops
versus the Buddhist nuns,
the rope barbed-wire,

the barbs razors. The nuns hold on
and squint like shocked florists,
the troops grimace like bug surgeons.

Both sides dressed clean: the soldiers starched,
the women yin-yang loose in black
and white...gain an inch, lose an inch.

Their long mule faces stretch
longer. The soldiers devil snort,
the women serpent-hiss static.

Both sides tippy-toe back and forth,
each side more pissed
that the other can't see urine is gold...

good folks at home, perhaps, picnic
citizens, but showing Christ's bloody hands
today and blinking swastikas.

HOT MONK AND COOL DOG

(June 1963)

Thich Quang Duc sits himself
down like kindling and prays,
out in the middle of the street,

a death-row crash-test boulevard
from bikes to tanks,
playing kamikaze like rats on speed,

then here's this monk,
this human marshmallow fallen
in his own flames,

this Superman
flashing a cape of smoke
over Saigon.

Off to his side, a dog sits in
the frog
position, belly on the ground,

front legs
out straight like railroad tracks,
back legs

bunched alongside the hips
grasshopper style. He licks
a front foot like a scoop

of ice cream. Can't help but notice
his tongue same as Clark Kent's,
a small wet flame.

THE DI ANN MARKET DALMATIAN

(June 1963)

A living dog is better than a dead lion.

Di Ann's elders fail to pay Nguyen
the rice tax needed to topple
Saigon. There they eat Uncle Ben's.

Results, a bamboo basket filled
with nails blows Di Ann's marketplace,
three or four people killed,

dozens wounded, kids tossed
like a Caesar's salad. Death has
that terrible sweet tooth

for olive eyes
and long green thumb
for casket wreaths.

After the dust and crumbs
settle, all Nguyen must do
to make Di Ann whimper and jump

through burning hoops
is leave a mysterious basket in
the market. Mom and dads skid stop,

think of the youngster torn
so badly his shadow
looked like a Dalmatian.

RICE MAN AND WATER BO GO TECHNO

For that which befalleth the sons of men befalleth beasts...they have all one breath.

The rice man and his water bo straddle
the fence, pay rice tax to both sides,
and it's turning them Vegas colorful.

Saigon tells rice man tote the rice
like a bunny, for camouflage. He hops
ball-shredding down the fence.

Hanoi says haul ours like a black
top hat—so no one sees (as you straddle the fence)
what's up your sleeveless cuff.

Water Bo also hopes to please
using his horns
as a trapeze

bar—turns
flips, flies, and moos
pink pastel scarves from either end.

Back at the hooch,
call it a day, drop two aces
in the toaster, see what pops up.

MADAME NHU PLAYS HERSELF

   (June 1963)

Wears a chandelier-size necklace,
lavender debutante
gloves, and Hell's Angels sunglasses.

She's the First Lady of South Vietnam
and can't decide if she is really General
Electric, a <u>Playboy</u> Playmate, or Puritan,

her bunny tail
cut from Revelations, so there
is no scandal.

She's here to inspect Saigon's first-ever
female fighters, fatales in French
catwalk couture...killer diller

pants tight as panty-hose
and large headgear
like Renoir's ladies in Paris.

These Mexican-French sombreros,
just what Nam needs to save
the war from becoming about berets.

The Renoir lids get rave
reviews—whoa Buddha Cutee, tres bien,
hotdamn babee zehr gut, tu craze

moi luv. But Madame Nhu preaches brimstone
hell forever when the girls want
their war cleavage showcased on *Cosmopolitan*.

Madame Nhu decrees, NO WOMEN MAY DANCE,
FRENCH KISS, SUCKEE SUCKEE, FREQUENT MOTELS,
WEAR MINI-DRESSES, OR DIVORCE.

Nothing American! although ladies
who blindfold Madame Nhu with cash
may have their eyes Liz Taylorized.

FLAG VEX

> **A man hath no better thing under the sun, than to eat, and to drink, and to be merry.**

Saigon rips down the Buddha's flags.
Can't everybody see? A flag is a nation's
official bowling shirt, one silk for all.

Let Buddha keep his flag, then everyone
wants his own flag to flap. Who'd stop
whorehouses waving poontang-nation pink?

So, the pagodas stand flagless as Catholic
church spires. But not long. Buddha stinks
up the whole town. Can't stop a monk

from raising his flag in the breeze.
He's got that head bald as a match
and wears kerosene robes.

His smoky rag unfurls fifteen minutes.
It's Buddha's tallest flag,
seen worldwide on the evening news.

Plus, word of mouth. Tongues flap
like grand-opening pennants,
"Monk delicacy that comes burnt."

And from the clouds, Buddha
smiles down, belly a bowling ball,
Yall let the good times roll.

BUDDHA TOURIST AGENCY

   Remove sorrow from thy heart.

When Buddha smells a monk
torching himself,
sees a body erupt

into a bush of thorny flames,
a human rose
that bigod eats itself—

Buddha rocks back and yuks.
The flames, those high-octane
hissers, are how he sticks

his tongue out at Saigon
and nanner nanners their gizmos,
their napalm and Phantoms.

Then he resumes the smile to show
Mona Lisa it should
be sweet and sour, balanced pork.

That smile is also his loveboat canoe.
It's how he floats above it all.
Get fat on Buddha's Skinny Cruise.

Forget the Molotov Cocktails,
too sweet, and Zippo juice
too sour. Eat love, throw rice.

EXAM FOR TANK KIDS

(November 1963)

Nam isn't a pagan
country. But God here is
lazy. Take elections.

President Diem loses
by two bullets. Though as
a vote that's close,

outside the Palace gates students
cheer a landslide, from on
top of a tank, all in white shirts,

packed so tightly the tank
turret looks like a white
rose swaying in the wind.

The kids all tilt
one way—whoopsie—almost fumble
themselves, then catch

their weight and fall
backwards. Balanced on a pinhead,
they could possibly fail

to recognize the tank's
a steel rug and the next
president Ding Dong just

might yank this steel carpet
from under them,
as did the little Jesus prick,

President Diem.
History repeats itself,
so God keeps on

blowing the dust
off the revolution exam
and giving it again.

THROW NGUYEN'S ASS OUT
ON THE DANCE FLOOR

It is good and comely for one to eat and to drink, and to enjoy the good of all his labour.

Nguyen won't blow up. We're wasting bombs.
Let's flatten him with red Corvettes,
mom's apple pie, white sport coats, and

Sansabelt slacks. Rip up the pine caskets
and hammer dance floors out of them. Tracers
for neon lights. Chopper fans. Beat

howitzers into Wurlitzers, sniper
cross-hairs into crosses.
bullets into birth-control pills. And for

each man, a PLAYBOY bunny for lunches,
something to bounce
home to, taps flashing on his heels.

And Nguyen's sport coat? Maybe we can't
go a loud red Karl Marx carnation, but,
sure, I think we can go a little pink.

GULF OF HONKY TONKIN

(August 1964)

A Jimi Hendrix screeching night—
lightning spiders climbing, whitecap tombstones
crashing...skull blop, skull blip...

can't see doodly shit, torpedo
zeroed on us or not?
and long as a telephone pole.

We got sonar hi-jinx or what?
pinball electricals...
Commie gunboat sniffing our freak?

Or what? The US ships report: "No actual
sightings by Maddox...Turner Joy reports
no wakes...many doubts." LBJ says, "Bull

shit. They're plowing us six feet deep
out there. Sonar beavers, my ass. Ho Chi
Minh's Halloweening us. He thinks

I'm some dumb-bunny Texas twink
and don't know chop sticks from flip-flops
from clip clops from clip joints.

But, my fellow Americans, let's get
this straight: I let Uncle Ho pull
my dick, next he'll yank down my underpants.

Give him Southeast Asia? Next, he'll
think his pecker is long as mine. It's hump
or be humped, who is the camel?

It's time, dammit,
to nail Ho's ding
dong to the clock.

Today, he's shooting Wayne
Newton the bird. Who tomorrow?
Be feeling-up John Wayne.

MOTHER EARTH MESSES WITH FATHER TIME

Better is an handful with quietness, than both the hands full with travail and vexation of spirit.

Nam, North and South, is a bosom
boutique geographique,
graves here mounded like breasts,

three-foot tall earth titties
spilled everywhere. Mother Nature braless,
burnt that bridge long ago. Pisses

off Father Time in his new Lamborghini hearse,
can only creep
forward, pitching a fit, stomping the brakes.

What use the sputnik gas?
The skull hood ornament?
The sneer trajectories?

The titty mounds unite
all Vietnam into the world's
biggest speed bump.

DADA NAM

Vinh Linh (North Viet Nam),
seen from the air, lies there like art,
acres on acres of discount Cezanne,

those fuzzy rectangles and squares
in washed-out greens
and grays. Until we add

our TNT idea, and dark brown
circles pock the landscape. Before
our splatter art goes down,

this rice-box Cezanne wasn't worth
fifteen cents an acre. But now that we've
invested half-a-million bucks

in it, it's not worth a dime. Wherever
we go, the Vietnamese leave...
look down their long faces like we're

art-goober hillbillies.
They fathom Da Vinci's
Mona Lisa deeper than we

do. They'll tell you her world famous
smile ain't turd compared to Buddha's
quietly joyful, if not jovial, puss.

And they can tell you why. Because
Mona Lisa's an Italian redneck,
who cut the world a silent poot,

lifted leg up and let off a garlic
stinky for the ages, and that
smile — she's just gotten the first whiff.

Nguyen thinks: bombers today, what next?
Mobile homes with their Elvises
humping the wall, watched by gay Jesuses?

THE ROMANCE OF THE CLEAN MARINES

(March 1965)

Marines unass the ship—
weapons oiled, prayers stuttered—
and assault Danang Beach...

hair all Dippity-do'd,
pits Spiced,
and teeth COLGATE'D should

the Pearly Gates open. But what? Vietnamese
beauties smother them with applause and noose
their necks with fragrant necklaces,

leis made of red gladiolas
and bright yellow dahlias.
Each grunt's got 600 bullets,

there to defend his chopped Chevy's fuzzy
dice in Texas. The Commies get
them, they might haul ass him to Vegas.

But GI Joe's lucky. The leis around his neck
bless with the luck of a flower
horseshoe. But something isn't right.

Or isn't it? These slinky chicks in their
party pajamas...smiling like Spring Break.
What's wrong is we got rifles everywhere,

but not one ukulele plinka plinks.
Plus, this beach smells
like a fat chick on a blind date.

WHITE NIGHTGOWN FLOWER ARIA FOR MEN

> There is no remembrance of former things; neither shall there be any remembrance of things that are to come.

Nam's National Flower is the Vidalia
Onion. Peeled of its white nightgowns,
in its center a tear Made In America.

Oh, horny honeymoon,
oh men, why must you peel
off the nightgowns?

SERGEANT DEATH GOLFS BOB

A chopper landing whacked a guy's head off
so clean he didn't fall for a moment,
a headless statue upright as a golf

tee. Or, more like
golf pole
with dripping flag.

And just last month, Bob Hope,
same chopper pad,
hit a chip shot and posed.

PIGGYVILLE PORKS AWHILE

Two teenage pigs, Porky and Miss Peaches,
were gifts from Arkansas. We escorted
these two lovebirds to a tiny village

famous for its honeymoon shed
and big ooze pool.
Mr. & Mrs. Ham had a whole mud

Versailles for the genealogical
future of pork.
The poor folks in the ville

would turn into fat cats selling piglets—
buy radios and eat like Mama Cass,
swap their buffaloes for golf carts.

Two weeks later we check on Mr.& Mrs.
Whoopee, see if their loblolly
still smells like fresh toe-cheese.

Are their party tails still curly?
We heard no pig patter, no Oink
we want our slop? We found their whirl

pool congealed, unstirred, covered with
an iridescent sheen. The pork
project had been eaten because they ate

too much, would rather eat than poke.
So, the comrades threw the village a barbecue:
chitlins, spare ribs, shoe soles,

pork chops. The tails made glue
and soap. The hides, leather luggage—
great for excursions to Moscow,

Peking, or Havana. The whole village
cheered, "We like having these choices.
Please send two more democracies."

AMBUSH MOVIE: SURPRIxE, JANE FONDA

Nguyen has this movie which he sneaks
around and shows in the most unusual
places—draws a crowd without pubic-lip

ventriloquists or casual knife in
the ribs. Nguyen calls
his film **SurpriZe**. His friends

can't wait. They're hiding off the trail.
Their tunnel view allows
them to see only the American's ankles.

Racquel, down the road, flirts with Bob
Hope, while Nguyen waits beneath his bush
and leeches give him a blow job.

Nguyen waits till he's eyeballing GI boots
tromping. The first surprise is Nguyen
has no projector or screen, uses bursts

of tracers, flickers like old porno film.
The GIs do Frank Sinatras
and swan-dive for the dirt. They roll

behind the trees. They are the stars.
Some play mummies, some blink,
some grin at heaven like gargoyles.

And before the calvary choppers in
to take Nguyen's scalp,
one more surprise—Nguyen's gone,

up and dropped the curtain—
no dead or wounded left
behind, no shell casings, nothing.

All that remains is where Nguyen must
have been hit—a blood stain
in the shape of a weasel's face. It just

looks like a stain. It's not. It's Jane
Fonda's brown scarf.
Jane's always on the side that wins.

THE JUMPIN JACK FLASH PADDY

Waiting for the choppers,
we boogie to "Jumpin Jack Flash"
and strum our M-16 Stratocasters.

No Mick Jaggers here. Each of us
is Keith. The cigarette dangles.
We frown cat-fight faces.

When we raid the village,
I say, "Boys, don't hit my weenie,
I'm here to feed leeches."

The bullets hiss and ping,
while I shiver.
No need of body bags to keep

us rockers warm. Don't sack me in rubber
luggage. We're into girls and cool.
I'm fine till the mortars get us zero'd.

Then, I turn cold, my root shrinks small
as thread; and on my body bag, a stitch
starts inch-worming a name on the lapel:

JOHN DOE. John Doe? Wait, halt, I'm Keith.
Let's all get our faces on straight.
I'm the one with the dangling Lucky Strike

laced with Cambohdy Red.
Nothing like weed to help forget
you're just another pretty face.

FOG DOGGIE STYLE

> **Thou knowest not what is the way of the spirit...
> the works of God who maketh all.**

Fog — Nguyen's cotton candy, valley
full of it. It's his vase,
slips around in like a genie.

He drives it like a tank,
creeps quiet as Braille,
gets in on us so tight

we're a huddle,
a goal-line stand. But where's
Nguyen and the ball?

He might tie my shoelace.
I might hear that. I'm bent
double by my ears weight.

I'm the All-American center in
my stance, and Nguyen's the quarterback,
so on top of me, he's got my hard on.

NORTH VIETNAM TURNAROUND

Our bombs touch smack
splat on the oil jackpot—fireballs—
a dozen storage tanks,

smoke tumbling tall
and billowing
prettier than the Alps,

and then up swoops a SAM, a phone
pole tricked with fins,
but we aren't home.

We roach swerve to out-gun
Fate's call.
Fortuna wants our buns—

or Nguyen does, his finger,
about to roto-root
up our sphincter.

No sweat, we got a blink,
plenty of time to make our jet,
our locomotive, scoot

into a crack and slide on back
to Happy Hour: to cheap
beer, darts, and free peanuts...

plenty of time to wink at Fate,
one whore to another,
us both working the same corner.

GRENADE HAMLET CALAMITY

> He that observeth the wind shall not sow; and he that regardeth the clouds shall not reap.

Nguyen rolls the hand-grenade
under your balls, not mine (for example).
You stand there like Hamlet

and can't unmuck, whether to haul
ass or pick up the frag and chunk
it back and let Nguyen stall

and wonder where's his hat, and what
the fuck? It Hamletmatizes
you—can't act because you can't stop

thinking, freezes
your feet, the frag hissing between
them like dry ice.

But there you are, the Hamlet hen
sitting on a bad egg,
Farmer Nguyen counting your chickens.

Unham your philosophing ass
or get blown up in the last scene,
with only Nguyen the audience.

Move it, Hambone, can't dream
life's a trout stream just because Nguyen
tossed you a can of worms.

FLIES SING COPPERTONE

If you sleep in the sun
too long in Nam, you'll get
the Saigon tan,

a blue iridescence
Coke-bottle green.
And there's that hiss,

though no air's escaping.
Bt you are swelling up.
Sounds like water boiling.

But can you be that hot?
Flies fan you down
though you got frozen feet.

PHANTOM JET SKY DOODLES

The Phantom squats—a three-legged insect,
blasting a Darlington 500 hurricane,
but compact as a wart.

Once it's airborne,
it loops-out curlicues,
twirling Nguyen a Dear John,

flourishes a message
to Nguyen that this here jet's
about to kick your ass.

Nguyen answers back
with his shovel and carves
a tunnel type of script,

miles of underground curlicues,
his note back to the jet.
Kicka butt, eh? I kicka yours.

Sky-curlicues versus earth-curlicues—
two cats going at it, each with a ball
of guts another day further unrolls.

GREENERY d'NAM

d'Nam is all
green possibilities.
From jade monkey jungle

to Buddha's emerald mahoganies,
to paddy-flat diarrhea lime
to China Sea chartreuse.

What greenery. From celadon toe-jam
and Asian aqua marmalade,
to body-bag marine.

And don't forget the shade
Nguyen wears on his brow as
Uncle Ho's mortuary CPA.

You know this awning's cheap because
not made of green plastic,
made from avocado peelings.

Nguyen gets into your mouth,
he's slime sliding up your sweet tooth.
He's everywhere, like dirt—

dollar bills on his feet.
You scratch your head and look—
Nguyen grows on trees.

MEKONG LUCIFER COOL

All things come alike to all.

The Saigon and American
flags sag lifeless at equal heights,
this sauna afternoon—

droop like tropical fish
who've gotten stuck
on the devil's pitchfork.

Nothing stirs. Humidity thick
as wet concrete, each breath
a blowtorch suck.

Nam's where Lucifer takes
his vacations, loves to snorkel
here in the human cloaca,

enjoys a napalm spritz,
reads fireman manuals, and blows
hot-tar double bubbles.

Got too many snowballs
in hell—might catch a cold—
so comes here to relax.

HOSPITAL VAMPIRETORIUM

The parents try to comfort their teenage
daughter. She's lost a foot, how kick field goals
for Yale? Mom and dad swab her brow, two canaries

cooing the blues, all their tender gestures
weaving a cage around the girl they can't
enter. She pats their hands. A nurse

gauzes her nub. And soon
her stump's a Q-
Tip strong enough to stomp

around on a clean floor. Now, who'd
have thought a janitorial career
hers? Mom and dad cheer, as she could

be lying there minus both feet
like a two-legged fork.
She could have lost both legs,

actually, be a peanut
with arms. No, she's Sister Ahab
and walks past the goal post.

She thumps
the deck...her pulse pompoms,
send short skirt and small underpants.

SKI VIETNAM TODAY OR TOMORROW

Ski Indochina. Snow
so cheap you score it by the Alp.
Why lie awake with skull

and crossbone thoughts,
sweating like a bottle
of iodine. A tiny snort

of Bach Bien turns any jungle
into Iceland, grenades
into snowcones, bayonets—popsicles.

Ski where the virgin snows
drive you into effortless trim,
can deeply fuck yourself

without even your palm
reader flogging you crystal balls.
Ski sunny Vietnam.

LINES OUT THE BOO HINEY

That which is crooked cannot be made straight.

Line up for your tetanus
and plague shots. Line
up outside the whore house.

Parade in lines out to the plane.
Line up, numbnads. Line up to leap
out of a door and yell AIRBORNE.

Line up in coffins for your trip
to mom—tears ruining her Revlon
cheeks, fall in straight lines. Shift

your weight like an accordion.
Please wait in line
for your army-sucks inoculation.

Should it fail, go back to end of the line
and wait. How long? No clock
in Nam. Each gooning neck's a metronome

correcting time. Now let's assault
Nguyen's ville. Form columns, hump
No Man's Land till you're lost

and can't tell your footprints
from those left by the Japanese,
Chinese, Mongolians, and French.

Just follow their long lines.
They're sheep no insomniac
counts. Nam's a limp tombstone

in the shape of an old man's dick.
But nations can't wait to line up
and scratch their obituaries on it.

BEER JESUS

There is no good...but for a man to rejoice, and to do good.

We're choppering along, loaded
with Christmas beer for the snuffies—
a flying keg, a St. Bernard

whirling. The stork hauling Baby Jesus
was not a better do-gooder. Three beers
and the mug turns into stained-glass.

More people ought to do good more
frequently. We do not forget
our small friend, Nguyen, either.

We drop him two six-packs
and *Playboy's* Miss Universe.
Pray flog his mule in peace.

The glory of Falstaff,
our gift to Nguyen. Tomorrow let him burn.
Today pour him a crown.

LOVERBOY ROSES BY HOWITZER

All toil and all skill in work come from one person's envy of another.

We fire off sixty-pound roses at the jungle —
harassment shells, shoot on a hunch
Nguyen's gondoliering down Romance Canal.

Kill him and his lovebabe, or bomb a fish,
the big red flash discourages traffic.
Nguyen's likely off shaking down the Chinese.

But there's a chance we'll pop his ass
while he's picking which skeleton
to wear out of his closet of tuxes.

Some think we shouldn't try to pin
explosions on Nguyen's childlike chest,
a worm so catshit poor he bums

off even Yugoslavia. But he's
a James Bond swank, formal. Not even Hugh
Hefner has more black silk pjs.

FNG THE VANILLA GRRR

Fucking new guy—this lieutenant,
El Tee Love Stud, a pro halfback,
maybe—flexes vanilla-scoop biceps,

exhibits the surf-board stomach,
elbow nose...sweat
clinging to the back of his shirt

makes the shape of a cross. And El
Tee—Mister Football— wants to score.
But Nguyen has all the balls.

And there are no goal posts
in Nam. Only the cross leaking on El
Tee's back. Problem, how punch

a ball, which you don't have, over a goal
Nguyen keeps behind your back? El Tee
stumbles, hauling around all that muscle,

not to mention the cross he wears daily
on his back. He's worse off than Jesus, who also
carried a goal post, but his folks kindly

kicked him through in three days. Who knows
how long our vanilla gorilla must tote
his cross before the spikes grab hold?

NUMBNUTS CONSIDERS BAYONET

The heart of the sons of men is full of evil, and madness is in their heart while they live, and after that they go to the dead.

If you haul ass,
the sergeant advises Numbnuts,
then you're the puss,

and champagne Nguyen
will slice your ass like cake,
a pigstick honeymoon.

You've also got a bayonet,
the one, unless your mind
is fucked, you do not beat.

Slip it in Nguyen's blind
eye, before he slips you his.
One of you is the bride.

ONION MOUTH SPEAKS WAR FACE

Wherefore, war is an onion that
keeps peeling itself, saving face
until there's nothing left.

TRENCHES AND PETTICOAT COMBAT

Ruffles around a hill,
that's all trenches
are to colonels—

ruffles, fringes,
mere necklaces
to dress a hill.

Dig in, dig deep, ladies.
Naw, oops, pack up, wrong hill,
move out, go west, go east.

Ditches, that's all
trenches are, new wrinkles
on an old skull,

some wiggly lace.
Colonels
think hills are breasts,

a thrill a hill.
Take that nipple.
If God didn't

want numbnuts to shovel,
why'd He give him blisters,
instead of gloves?

AGENT ORANGE, ORANGE CRUSH, NO PROB

> There is no remembrance of former things; neither shall there be any remembrance of things that are to come with those that shall come after.

The plane sprays Agent Orange
a quarter-mile away. Birds tweet,
bugs curl, I feel red-eyed myself.

We're like a caterpillar with
our head stuck in the mist,
and our tail telling us no sweat,

the lieutenant
back there, our head and ass
lost in the map.

What if ten years from now my nose
looks like a butterfly,
you dig? my weenie a weeping willow?

What if I sneeze? What if I go crazy
and turn into an oak
full of owls and get a nasty

cough, yelp like a worn-out
chain saw? Say, one morning
I go HOOT HOOT and hack

myself right off the limb
Uncle Sam had me crawl out on?
I'm saying, what if in fifteen

years I'm home and shaving, trying
not to behead my Monarch nose, and I cough and
my dick falls off? Who'll come running?

A shrink
waving a net or tree
surgeon?

POETS COMMIT HIGH BARD

For in much wisdom is much grief.

Poetry in this war
is published on helmets.
Shaky Shakespeare

won't print his ditties on toilet
walls, while his balls
swing over a barrel of cesspool creep.

Will scribes all his haikus, riddles,
and oracles, and telegrams
where they'll be seen, on the bubble

atop his head — I SCREAM ICE CREAM,
NO HUMPING PLEASE, SEE TIT
CITY OR BUST, DON'T MEAN NOTHING.

What else would you expect
to drink truth serum but poets?
The officers don't scratch

headlines on their helmets.
Too public, like condom
sharing. They're fictionists,

Nobels for flatulence,
and Pulitzers
for writers' blanks.

PRIVATE HOLLYWOOD VEGAS

At Monsieur Death's Boutique,
should you get your trigger hand shot
off, he'll throw you a hook

so you can still salute.
You lose an eye? Select
yourself a marble wink.

Don't despair, Dude. What luck.
Hook and glass eye, you're Mr. Hollywood,
and Vegas writes the script.

Casinos pop from sand to croon and woo
losers to play your pirate role.
Son, you are the real Popeye, you're

the dude the slots all roll
their eyes at, how you cheated death
and now buy their one-arm salutes.

TIMEX PUGILISTES

Nguyen blows his bugle and overruns us.
I play possum and let him take
my boxing-glove ring, peace symbol, and watch.

When he raises my wrist, my breath
goes flat. My testicles
skid like snails from his bayonet.

Otherwise, I play dead so still
my pulse, all waving flags, all the planets
all go into instant deep freeze.

I concentrate till cold and stiff
as a dead bass, then realize my eyes
should be open if I'm a fish,

should be two dull marbles
done with rolling,
two crystal balls made of tin foil.

If I'm confused, imagine Nguyen thinking:
This dude can't be no world champ Ezzard Charles.
But Nguyen's raises my hand like I've just won

the rice world heavyweight title,
holding my hand by the fingers
like a shy referee. He unbuckles

my watch so slowly I wonder
if he's reading my palm. He thinks
I've knocked myself out forever.

ADMIRAL BEETLE TELLS GENERAL BEETLE

Be not righteous over much: neither make thyself over wise.

The problem, mon General, is this fort
where we stand—made of dirt,
this fort shaped like a boat—won't float,

though Nguyen wants inside it.
And why shouldn't he? B-52s plop
holes around it as big as fish

ponds. I tell you, mon General, the fort
has no better chance of sailing
than a dirt boat made out of dirt.

Logic. Plus, when the Nguyens pile in,
it's got to sink. That's more logic.
And then what, we'll march right back in

and build it back with more logic,
this ark of mud. And they'll come back
all diddybop to once again sail it

with more logic. How beat a lick
of sense into the hat
Nguyen stole from Admiral Zumwalt?

THE GUARD REPORTS SEEING THE LIGHT

Dog blackass night...my eyes
two rat
holes stuffed with dynamite.

Sword in my guts, not knowing what
Nguyen's up to—night tai chi
or shadow kick-boxing, or chewing Certs?

I'm bright-eyed as Liberace.
I fall asleep
and wake to find a purple French

tickler. It sheaths
the end of my rifle.
One of Nguyen's jokes?

He is the kind of guy who'll bowl
your ankles with a skull. This sleeve,
this rubber on my rifle could

be a buddy's, showing how easily
Nguyen could sneaky-pete up and blow
dry my wet dreams in a twinkle.

Or this prank might be the work of
the company fairy, Merlin, purple
his color, hails as a Knight of

the Round Table. Wants my candle...
his tongue the flame.
Close as Nam gets to a castle.

I'm not that kind of king.
If anything circles my head
I want my ears showing.

JOKER REPORTS
UNPLEASANTNESS OVERCOME

I starve. I try to nap. The guys
play poker and goof off.
I make-believe their noise

is nothing, that the flutter of
the shuffled deck
is a quail covey taking off

from a Thirteenth
Century field, flushing
out of a meadowlark

meadow in Merry Olde England.
Soon, I get a surprise—.
A carriage nears. It's Queen Elizabeth

inside, with a banana split
for me made of breasts.
Then more dealing of cards. That swish

sliding on the table, that's Her Highness
rustling her petticoats and plucking the ruby
from her navel. That come-here gaze.

She drops it like a wild cherry
between her breasts, whitest double mirage
ever to rise from a shithonk paddy.

Why are we here? Why fight for rice?
Rice stunts your growth, is fertilized
with human waste, and makes your eyes

squint even when dead. We won't even try
to win. We fight only for apple pie.
America is the dessert country.

THE VIETNAM PIN-UP CALENDAR

Your calendar in Nam,
right here, a naked girl with 365
small blank tombstones

on her body. Days you don't die,
slash a black X on one of your
tombstones. Seems like

that tombstone wasn't yours
today. Start X-ing out
on the extremities of her

beauty and work
haphazardly
in toward the clamp:

X-off a big-toe nail
one day, ear lobe the next.
Be unpredictable,

fuck-up
perfect
fuck-ups.

Never take the same trail twice. Nguyen
spies every Lovers Lane,
and he won't even give you time to bend

over. No, wait a minute. Don't
start X-ing out on the fringes
of your lady. First day, go on

and ink your X
on her cherry. She's your
Virgin Mary,

and you're her boy
each day you mark
your cross on her body.

B-52 BOMB CREEP

The work of God, that a man cannot find out.

It flies so high you can't see or
hear it...black hole
in space with green-eyed computers,

it's the rooster raptorus of shitnails,
carpet-bombing that lights
Nguyen up all philosophical,

except when a bulls-eye turns him to mist.
Sometimes he's told to scram by Russian boats
trawling off Guam, fishing for flights.

But sometimes Nguyen gets zapped
by only the concussion, leaves
him sitting, a custard in thought.

B-52's are extremely unConfucius.
They zap without the courtesy
of tapping you on the shoulder.

BUNKER CAT QUICKEES

If built
out of concrete,
it's French.

Pierre
thought he would fight
Nguyen forever.

If built
of sand
bags, it's

American, sliding
through the hour
glass from day one.

This war
no more than a
summer...

America's
quick war,
McNamara's

jiffy McWar.
Order your fries
from your chopper.

True, the arches
aren't gold,
and the French fries

aren't French,
but the United States
of America has

picnic experts —
eyes lemons and Nam's one
long sugar beach.

THE SNIPER SOUVENIRS GI

The sniper's bullet pings
near my left knee. The earth tingles
like one giant funnybone.

One bang and I grow eyes,
instant potato head,
with eyes on top of eyes.

I am insect twitchy, frog-eyed,
and wave elephant ears, but can't locate
Nguyen, while my head

swells into a fatter target.
Run? Don't jump? What? Jump up
and get plugged in the back?

Each breath my lungs like hot
air balloons lift my head higher.
Yes, I am a Catholic,

eyes rolling like prayer
beads. And the longer I sit on
my prayer balls, that's the longer

Nguyen has to squeeze a round
and harden my next birthday cake
into an Arlington tombstone.

Dive in the ditch? Stay put
behind the hooch?
Another pop. In one ear, out

the other. Who's the pussyfoot
Nguyen wants to souvenir? It's four
of us. The bird Nguyen throws

he keeps on his trigger,
no stiff straight-up fuck you,
but curled into a question mark.

Now aimed at who?
This finger curled
in the sniper salute.

PECKER NOSE CUSTOMIZE

We're glad Nguyen's dead if that photo in his
pocket is his wife, got the hippopotamus
nose. Lucky, won't see her face, now he's

lost his last lunch;
but in the photo, she grins like
all he needs is a crutch.

Her signature and note
at the bottom puzzles
our intelligent group.

Our blues singer believes
her name is Miss Yo Dick,
and a symposium ensues:

"My Ass," retorts our gynophysicist.
"Naw, Yo Mama," responds our genealogist.
And Spaghetti, our Mafia plastic

surgeon, says, "Her name is
Cuckoo," and cuts a hole
in the picture where Miss

Yo Dick's nose was,
then pulls
Nguyen's trouser mouse

through it. We all agree she's prettier
with the Pinocchio nose, but wonder,
our Dear Abby does, if she's a liar.

Our Hollywood lawyer wants to send her
a bill. We saddle up and leave Miss Yo
updated, courtesy of Nguyen's pecker.

Last year hippo
the latest look,
this year rhino.

VALENTINE'S DIRTY DAY

The jet has six voodoo bombs strapped
on it. Each one's a dirty tear
drop with a word scrawled in lipstick:

BEWARE OBJECTS ARE
CLOSER
THAN THEY APPEAR.

These heart throbs go
out to Nguyen's Virgin Mountain cave-complex.
He's got it honeycombed

with R&R love shacks.
Nguyen's not quite the prudish
old maid we'd thought.

Some caves have tubs of Holiday Inn trash,
from candy condoms to Tampons.
Nguyen's so mousy he hides even garbage.

The top and bottom of Virgin belong
to us, but the middle is Nguyen's ice house,
and far too slippery for our men.

Serve Nguyen his eviction notice
at one hole, and he'll grease
you in the back from another.

Best way to reach him is by jet,
that million dollar key. But where's
the door. The jungle door, no lock

on it, a big green wall with no hinges.
All the pilot can do is drop his six powder
puffs and, if lucky, stir the dust in Nguyen's

guest suite, break the magic fingers.
Only to find out later all the Nguyens
there that week were chiropractors.

NGUYEN FREAKS HITCHCOCK

We GI's wear same clothes for weeks:
eat, sleep, die, and wet dream in them,
shit fire in them when your ass weeps

diarrhea. Not Nguyen.
He's Abercrombie & Fitch clean,
his hut neat as a nun's.

But when he gets his hands
on our trash rags, he gets funny
and turns them into an

Alfred Hitchcock trophy,
makes a GI scarecrow,
Dinky Dow #10.

For eyes got buttonholes,
rips scream, pockets
for sex, ears green lapels.

Shaped like a ball
and filled with straw,
it all but asks

who is more nuts,
Nguyen or Dinky?
Who gets more sex?

Who writes Nguyen's script?
Does fate erase?
Do not clothes make Hitchcock?

TET MAN A MESS

(31 January 1968)

It's Nam's July the Fourth, also its tooth
fairy, Christmas, and Halloween
all rolled into one New Year's Eve blow-out.

Certainly the case this year. Turns
out some pre-Tet coffins got packed
with Nguyens breathing through tubes,

waiting corpse cozy for the nationwide assault,
then up they rose like a navy of haints.
Just like Nguyen to use coffins for U-boats —

pop-tart comrades in red arm-bands or white
shirts with the top button buttoned. Freezes
me to think how close I came to buying a plot

from one of these Commie Lazaruses,
me thinking all the noise was firecrackers.
The really big roar was Karl Marx,

his trick cigar — Ka BOOM — when there
was no nationwide uprising. The Nguyens
went on and threw themselves slaughter

parties, painted the towns red with their own
bugjuice. But whipped the USA. Mr. and Mrs. Bubba
authorized the White House to bring the boys back home.

It's time to quit fighting when a
graveyard yawns, and Westmoreland flicks
a flame-thrower to light his Havana.

Mr. and Mrs. Bubba had a point.
But Westy deserves his puff, too.
The Viet Cong were done, bell rung,

finis, boo coo boo hoo.
But TV at home showed for each
who dead another boo.

SLEEP LUCKY VIA HOT DAMN

If you can sleep without dreaming of Nguyen
throwing glass eyes at you, you escape Nam.
Sleep lucky and sleep-walking Nguyen

won't flip you the finger without an arm,
won't yo-yo your Adams
apple. Sleep deep and you slip out of Nam

onboard the world's oldest airlines,
HOT DAMN SWEET DREAMS: you're one lucky
mother, dreaming you're golfing with Janis

Joplin, tonguing her tiny tee,
her hand hoisting your flag
pole, you about to putt any

moment, go fourth-dimensional,
where your Z's exist but you don't.
Sweet dreams and you are sleep's black hole

in space, escaped from the donut.
Sweet dreams and no quicksand traps kill
your wedge; you're gone, you are the beach

escaped from the long white towel
of sand. Sweet dreams and you've a hole
in one, without touching your mule.

TUNNEL RAT FROGMAN

Danger is perfectly peter
hardening. Our Danny keeps a hard
on—Danny Mo, poontang diver,

down there rooting around
in Nguyen's bowels,
drunk on formaldehyde,

almost bumps into tiny clothes
hanging mid-air. Nguyen's junior bras?
No, sir, a clothesline of cobras

gliding in place,
Nguyen's Laundrymat
of cobra capes.

Now Danny Mo finds sunlight drab,
prefers worm world, with a flashlight,
and hooked to an adrenaline mask.

But why, you ask,
did his pubes turn
white over-night?

Once you dive into Mother Death's
snatch and resurrect back,
you're reborn with an undertaker's dick.

Might be Death's crotch,
chill and moldy,
but it never grows old.

NGUYEN'S FRIGHTENING OUCH

These GI's big-eyed as puppies,
hairy as rangatangs, hung with pythons,
lard-assed as water buffaloes —

they own the day in Nam.
The sun belongs to these Americans
same as kisses belong

to lips. But night belongs
to Nguyen like moons
belong to fairy tales,

like water buffaloes belong
to flies, like red-white-and-blue buffs
must jump through Nguyen's nose rings

nightly. Get bitten on the ass
nightly and per the nose ring cannot jump,
how long can a fellow yell Ouch?

The night belongs to Nguyen
like *Playboy* centerfolds
belong to Airbrush Man.

The day belongs
to GI's like soap operas
to ladies crying and yelling.

THE KITE GRENADE VOCALIZES NGUYEN

This kind of nerve torture
does involve sweat, with some horseplay,
but not always. Tie the prisoner's

hands behind his back and seat him in a
room you don't mind blowing up, on a stool.
Tie his feet. Place grenade in a

can (bangs when pulled
out of can). Put in the rafter.
The grenade kite, it's called,

string runs from the guy's ear
to the grenade. He listens. He can rat
on his red comrades or sit there

until he falls asleep and jerks
the frag down, which action turns his
nightmare into an alarm clock

with four seconds to tick
before it blows, unless
the grenade is a fake,

sucker. Who knows?
Gives tight-lipped Nguyen
a second chance

to sing. So, now, he can
tattle and still hold his head high.
He's proven he's a man.

He flew the grenade kite
without squealing? So, he's a man.
Few men, however, wish to fly it twice.

CAR BOMB TONY

I used this store's windows as my mirror
to check out my monkey shoulders,
short legs, balding spot, and big ears.

And my cap problem. Wear
the bill Mickey Mantle straight-ahead or
cocked upwards like Yogi Berra?

So, I'd look in this store's
windows to tell. My eyelashes
too short? Sideburns quarter

inch too long? And while I preened, these
windows were cannonballs loaded
with flying glass, packed down with stares

and blinks and yawns by both the good
guys and the shopping guerrillas.
I was two blocks away when a spring ticked

and the windows popped like bubbles.
People sailed and doll-flopped. The mannequins
smiled bright red lips, Pompeii postures,

one in a green shark-skin
Italian suit and Chinese hushpuppies,
doing the Australian

crawl, an Asian Tony Curtis,
big curly hair, smiling like an
Alcoholic Anonymous.

Compared to Mr. Curtis, I looked fine,
He mannequin or magician,
but no time to be bleeding, cut in half.

CAR-BOMB JITTERBUG

I'm wanting to buy mom a pearl necklace
with money I won playing cards. But fake
pearls or real, which ones are bogus?

My hair swoops forward from the back
of my head, a hurricane wave,
to cover my lack of hair luck on top.

When I study pearls in windows, my gaze
may trip
one of Nam's plate-glass guillotines,

and with a blast
of shards, slice me thin as
the King of Spades.

And how would mother recognize
me with my hair parted six ways
at once, and goodbye King of Spades.

I might win the shelf of toupees.
But what good if my smile
were parted the wrong way?

CAM RANH BAY HARD-ON

What a place. Pastel Crayola breezes,
silver sand dunes, the sun
a gold moon pie. Cam Ranh's you Key West East

and Vegas all-in-one Rear Echelon
Motherfucker (REMF) Paradise.
Got goofy golf, swimming, German

lager, lobsters, Zinfandel, lingerie,
and round-eyes. Cam Ranh's also the Fort Knox
of officers with brown noses,

of butt-snorkeling Major Mickey Mouses.
But if you don't mind burning shit barrels
and white-glove inspections—the rocks

snow white, everyone wears white-wall
haircuts—and if you like strait-jacket starch
and can salute all day like a windmill,

then C.R.B. is hard-on nirvana: Red Cross
nurses, Donut Dollies, and WACS,
and Waves. Bikini heaven at the beach—

Miss Lonely Heart from Arkansas,
Vermont's Miss Daisy Mae,
New York's Miss Puissance d'Fuzz...

all showing face
freckles, and butt dimples,
and peach cleavage—

smell Georgia, you're that close—
showing off every little thing,
but their Californias.

BOOM TOWN TROUT

Beside the garbage ditch, up springs
a shack colorful as a trout,
for scales flattened beer and pop cans.

The roof a blaze of Coke
cans. Seven-Up chimney. Back door—Orange Crush.
Front door Blue Ribbon Pabst.

Fast as you can say, "Pepsi," Chin's Whore House
pops up beside this shack. The Race Track Bar
None Grill follows. Then, more sheds and hutches,

all these closets bunched together
into a leaning, rickety,
heaving, tin-plated dinosaur...

which swallows more people daily.
Can't move, a huge
wreck with no steering wheel.

This pop-beer can complex
attracts old folks,
children, and amputees—

all those who have a hunch
the real thing's not Coke but Pepsi,
not Dodge but Chevy dice.

TAIL CAPITALISM AND MARX FOK U

At Duk Wuk ville, Johnny Pimp's the youngest
businessman. He's about six, pimps
for his sister: "Fok U boo coo," he chirps.

His logo is a small-fry twat he makes
joining the tip of his index
finger with the middle finger. He waves

this hand-sized billboard in your face.
In his other hand, a Fok U lizard
for sale. This creature really croaks

FOK U. So, the girl or
the Romeo lizard, "U buy, GI?" One will
cost two bucks, or both for

three, the whole sucking Do Whack ville
for five. The pint-size pimp's
sister will make your snake shrivel.

His erotic lizard will wipe
out your roaches and mosquitoes.
Buy both, give these children a break.

Help the ville's youngest prostitute,
send the ville's
youngest capitalist to school.

RELIGION GETS THE JOB DONE AGAIN

That which is to be hath already been.

All isn't stone-
age dumb in Vietnam.
Take religion.

When you whip off, your hand
reincarnates into Marilyn
Monroe: your vine and mind

blossom, and you're reborn.
Very modern and platinum blonde,
these ancient religions.

CURVE THE ORIENT

I peed beside my jeep, the road
a curve two inches deep in dust,
nothing for miles, bare paddy land.

I suspected it was the nothing that's
not true nothing but Zen
hocus pocus. And, smartly, I was right.

The dust sprouted between
my feet—a shot—I jumped and hit the ditch
while still standing.

I later hot-rodded through that
curve daily, held down by only my plume
of dust. That curve was my power closet,

my rooster booster, and my communion
wafer—"God let me win this Buddha 500,"
and my heart will be that one hand clapping.

THE GENERAL'S POTTY ISN'T
A HONKY TONK

Baskin Robbins—we call him, General
Hard Stuff—hangs back in our jungle
base camp and inspects the Colonel's

battalion. The Colonel
is nervous as a virgin, smiles
Dairy Queen curlicues.

The General stays overnight
sometimes and tuffs it with the troops.
The Colonel must erect

the General his own toilet,
his own lunar
office, with the crescent

marked on the door.
But this toilet's not your average
Private Abner

stink chapel, where men meditate—
Playboy left hand and playstick right.
No Zen donging for Daisy Mae

in this office. Too bright—the Northern lights
in the ceiling, and under the General's ass,
the Big Dipper blinks for a chamber pot.

But all's well if in the General's fudge
the Colonel finds his nose,
and not good if he finds Groucho Marx's.

THE BAND AND THE TALL BOY

The South Vietnamese Army
band honks,
flutters, and squeaks away

on bamboo flutes, trombones,
bird-bath tuba, and garbage-lid
cymbals. The conductor's baton,

an aerial, makes lightning zigs.
A teen—black shorts, no shirt—
listens, a bony kid. His shoulders stick

out bunched beneath
his skin like clay pigeons
ready for skeet

shooting. The kid pats one
foot for Saigon
and one for Ho Chi Minh.

Must decide soon,
if he's to have two right
feet or two left.

THE LIPSTICK WAR GEOMETRY

This Nam war's all about circles. Circle
the wagons, shoot, move out, draw another
circle. Here, we're playing marbles.

Korea and the two world wars, though, were
about lines. Push the crazees back—
latitudes, longitudes—bulldoze like a glacier

until the land is cleared and plant
the Old Glories. This Nam war though's about
circles. Take land and expand like

we're making a bulls-eye target
for Nguyen's practice.
We win, we're gone. The little shit

moves in. The little shit loves us.
We're on the phone, we love him back,
we call in our make-up artists—

and choppers come, woppity tee wop,
firing crimson tracers,
circling like lipsticking a mouth,

just one more circle, Nguyen's smiler,
where daily more
of our beer and blood disappear.

RAT MAN THE CAT MAN RAT

Daniel Rat Daddy cuts
his hair when he pleases. He's his
own guru. He's a tunnel rat—

Tarzan knife, filed teeth, red whiskers,
flashlight, stubby pistol, Bible, a cat
smile, camel neck and breath, and a spider's

silky touch. The light is to snap
on and blind Nguyen in his tunnel.
The train Nguyen never sees is Rat

Daddy's snub-nosed midnight special.
Nguyen's underground in a haystack,
then here's Rat, sure as a needle.

Rat keeps his Jesus hair braided
in a long stringy tail.
His calling card's a page

from the Book of Daniel.
The whores call him Samson.
When he gets almost killed,

he slips into a Steam & Cream
and comes out limp and bald,
then, like a cat, sleeps in the sun.

When his hair's long again, he braids
the tail and resumes his career
again inspecting Nguyen's subways.

Rat puts his safety in prayer,
Rat Man the Cat. He claims
prayer is how the Christian purrs.

VIDALIA SLIM NGUYEN DELIVERS

Say not thou, What is the cause that the former days were better than these?

Nguyen races an
onionmobile. GI's call him
Vidalia Slim.

Burns 100% bingbang.
Forget pit-stops, when runs
up hill runs down.

No flaps, no coon
tail, but has Chevy dice, has no mirror,
but plays George Jones.

Got spares
inside
of spares.

Vidalia Slim outside your door,
pizza grenade, don't take it personal,
Chevy dice but no steering wheel.

PICASSO PEAK, OR DALI'S, NOT GAUGUIN'S (BECAUSE)

Sits there nameless
(seen one nothing, seen all)
until Nguyen fires,

and we blast back—napalm
hoochie coo—till the peak looks like Charlton
Heston's face tore up by a hurricane.

Later, the peak looks like the man
in the moon, though the nose
at six o'clock looks like an ear at nine,

right out of two-face Picasso.
To our pilots it's a Jack O Lantern.
They bang into it, drunk as moths.

Or call it Salvador Dali Mountain:
above it the warped clock—the hands
airplanes melting above Gauguin's jungle.

THE PRICK 25 RADIO

It rides you piggyback, your baby god,
gurgles ROGER, several knob
noses. Some days its your lifeguard:

you're whirling into shock,
your eyes the white of spilled sugar,
your blood on the wrong side of your tee shirt;

but hold on, here's your egg-beater,
thanks to Roger, to swoosh you back to pills
and white sheets. But this same Roger

may order you to attack the jungle.
You hump in circles till you're jerked
up flat in Nguyen's punji palace,

on top a bed of spikes shellacked
with buffalo doodoo, and no
porno princess to lend a hand.

So, how live with the radio?
Kills you, saves you. It's a second
pecker telling you what to do—

another knob, and you're merely a man:
the one-eyed monkey in your pants
and now the blind one on your back.

US EMBASSY WALL, OF ALL THINGS

There the war sprung its leak —
Westmoreland's tongue,
nothing else plugging it,

gashed mouth of a concrete pumpkin,
Nguyens pouring through the hole,
slipping by Westmoreland flapping.

Two months ago, he'd said the Nguyens
were a snowball in hell and picked
his teeth with an ostrich wishbone.

The hole blew out
perfect for Westmoreland
to get in and inspect,

no need to stoop,
already bent double,
foot in his mouth.

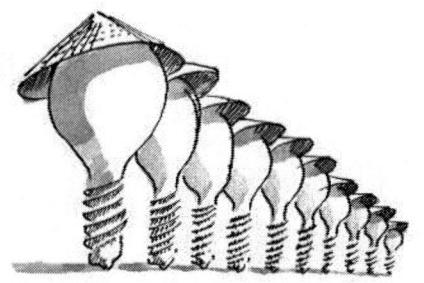

THE SAG IN YOUR COT IS PERSONAL

The rocket blew my tent
away and my comics.
I took it hard—the cot

where I'd wet-dreamed for months.
We were in love. My cot. No cot, no trace.
Could have been me, not just the sag

I'd pressed on the rotting canvas.
A sag's your body's signature,
your John Henry on the outer darkness.

My new cot sags like I'm an impostor.
Sags like I'm generic,
some kind of John Henry Doe or

a dummy without a ventriloquist.
I toss like a python scribbling.
Am I in the right script or not?

MY LAI AND THE SILVER PLATTER

(March 1968)

LBJ, the can-do cowboy,
ambles into My Lai,
and the kids and scarecrows

flatter him with their two-faced smiles.
They can play longhorn politics
too: grin or frown, the same toenail

paring. Their pigs grunt double talk,
as well, not the honest
HUT HUT of the U-Texas quarterback.

Puppet pigs and puppet
people, and in their grim
faces, LBJ sees his own cowpoke

self. So, he cuts their strings.
Four hours by the clock, but gets rid of
a lot of dusty frustration.

Four hundred drop. Enough
to make a Prez thirsty, pardner.
He slurps from the goat trough.

And there his face on the water
looks like a post-office
Wanted Dead Or Alive poster.

And what a huge surprise.
Lyndon is no Marlboro man smoking
a Clint Eastwood cigar.

LBJ's face on the tray of water
is Lieutenant William Calley's —
laid out on a silver platter.

LUCK OF THE BUTT

The grenade tore BB-size holes
in this guy's tail, ripped his buttocks
into cheese-grated bowling balls.

His buddy cheered him up,
"Your ass-scars, man, be stars
to women in the sack,

butt that lights up."
The wounded boy cruised on
planet Morphine. He did seem curious,

like life was Astronomy 001,
in which the Milky Way is a snowdrift
obscuring the constellations.

But, yes, a woman get a grip
on these bowling balls, got to roll
herself, later, a cigarette.

NAPALM FLORAL DE BOOM

For Nguyen's betrothal,
nothing beats a napalm bouquet,
as ordered by El Tee Beetle:

sends in the crimson-yellow buds
a la d'boom-de-boom kapoof,
followed by big black blooms

of smoke. Sniff that parfum
diesel jelly ablaze, just right
for Divine Comedy nuptials.

Nguyen gets what he deserves. The bride,
with Beetle as best man, doesn't show up.
But Nguyen comes running with the hard-

on of an all-night bayonet,
like a true groom, only to meet
the overhead florist,

the black
chrysanthemum
fireworks.

And Nguyen, our banzai groom,
wearing a crispy-critter tux,
finds he's in a smoky closet.

ARTY GOSH ALMIGHTY

2,000 feet high, we're hauling
four guys killed by friendly mortars,
wrong numbers kinda thing.

Also along, the butter-bar
who accidentally
called down the mortar fire.

He's heavy as the Titanic.
Can't quite admit life is mathematics,
can't say one plus x equals OOPS.

The clouds reflect the explosions
as pink roses, for a funeral-home
touch. Got no Hippie Jesus on

board, but a Jesus Nut holds the blade on.
The wind croons A&P Elvis,
and the Lieutenant's a bagpipe of groans.

But, heah, to goof is religious,
El Tee. Even Jesus,
God's own man with the bachelor lips,

screwed-up, back with Judas...
invited him to the banquet
and suffered his cold kiss.

Can't raise the dumbbell of regret,
El Tee, you're standing on it, El Tee. Walk
away. Even JC couldn't get his rocket

to lift off Calvary an inch
(Look, Mom, no hands). You want an OOPS,
El Tee, now that's your OOPS.

NEIMAN MARCUS NGUYEN POWERGLIDE

He once brown-nosed a water buff
twelve hours a day for rice
to grow, a plow-jockey in muck

knee deep, but he now wears quik-dry
footgear good as ours (but no berets
or swagger sticks or drum major

lances). Got the stronger grenade
launcher, the lighter pack,
his rifle bangs. Our Mattel jams.

Some dirt and it goes What.
Squeeze the trigger,
and you're pointing a stick.

Nguyen's poncho is superior,
also, doesn't reflect moonlight
and sheds the drops quieter.

Other than that, Nguyen's just a grunt,
another generic shitbird. He pulls
KP, needs more poontang in his diet,

locks heels when he salutes,
slips off AWOL, rinky-dinks like
we do, and what's really unique

isn't Nguyen's tiny hands or eyes
almonds blinking, but he's like us, fighting
to French kiss the ass he chooses.

THE PARIS PEACE TABLE SQUARES THE CIRCLE

(May 1968)

Okay, square like the Ping
Pong Dynasty's first table? Or
round as in square-dancing?

Perhaps, the round of moon-pies? Or
the longitudinal round of wieners?
Or globe-orb of flatass zero?

No, square like getting back to Square
One. So, now we're getting somewhere.
Square city block or square like a T-square?

Or square like the boxing ring? Or
round like the marriage ring? Opera
round—a prima donna's unibreast? Or

just roundish round like a pizza?
Or like the box it comes in—square?
We'll sit or stand, okay? That a

problem? Okay. Round like checkers?
Red checkers or black? Or,
what say, square like the checkerboard?

CATCHING BERNINI'S TROUT

This guy in shock looks like
a broken statue: face marble
white, fingers broken chalk,

his eyes daylight hopeful...
watches pigeon shadows
skim the fountain. They troll

like black topwater fishing lures.
Perhaps a trout will burst
up through the pool's mirror,

and the pigeon shadow will hook
it. This guys eyes show that
kind of arched-brow quizzical hope,

his eyes black pools of trust...
like he and Michaelangelo's
DAVID are rocking the same boat.

And why not play the ace
of hope? What's pigeon shit
but stone dandruff?

PLATO MEETS MA BELL AND

Nguyen's a card-carrying
Platonist, believes only in
ideas, not in dogs and cats and things.

His dead comrades aren't men,
but stepping stones toward Uncle
Ho's Buddha-Marx-Honda heaven.

Some torture electrons, though, did help Nguyen reveal
his top secrets—little thing of his testicles
hooked to a telephone. Each (non-Platonic) call

he got, he blushed more factual.
Thanks to Ma Bell, he dropped Platonism
and turned into Aristotle,

sang out of stool pigeons,
tunnel back doors, new maps,
and fall-back ammo dumps.

He, now, salutes the Saigon flag.
Does the lip curl? He's a red chameleon
writing the book on camouflage.

He's got the reptile brain.
His whole body is neck. His hat's a nest.
Whack him on the head, and

you get no knot, you get a Commie egg.
He's still a Platonist, except when Ma
Bell walks through his yellow pages.

THE WATER BUFF'S MUSTACHE DRAWS HIGH COMMENT

Doc's first assault
blundered in fog, a raid into
a robot-still village.

Major Frisbee, in the command chopper, was too
silent, too—dragonfly small in the clouds,
his eye not obscured by a closer view.

Doc took a purple fighting pill
to bob and dodge bullets.
No Nguyens, an empty ville.

Doc gulped a quiet-world pill
and punched the water buff,
For no reason. For general principles.

This stunned the buff. His mustache of
horn—worn on top
of his head—usually frightened off

all pugilists. But Buff thought fast.
A sweeping uppercut
knocked Doc sparkling like a Ferris

wheel. Child's play—Buff and Doc
recovered from their scrapes,
and Doc took home a Purple Heart.

Major Frisbee—leading the charge
from his fly-by hammock—
received Saigon's Astronaut Star,

and Buff shuffled-up to accept
the Teddy Roosevelt
Medal for best mustache,

though some generals thought
a mustache worn on top
the head not authorized.

ALICE, THE AIR MATTRESS

I'm out of ammo, so I lob a case
of Bud at Nguyen. When he chunks back
a grenade, I holler, "You piece

of dung, you've ruined my new cue stick,"
and fling a new pair of Converse tennis
shoes at him, the price tag flapping. He pops

up all adenoids and empties his
AK-47 and spits some words around.
I ought to stomp his bony ass,

but toss him a tub of popcorn
and my last Humphrey Bogart butt.
But can I get a light from Nguyen?

Oh, yes. He lunges with his bayonet.
I jump aside and hold up Miss
Playboy, catch his eye with her spiderweb.

The little idiot freezes,
dazzled by the blonde triangle
that racks Everyman's balls.

While he's blinking, I yell,
"Heah, Nguyen, trade a purple
Hi-California umbrella

for the red star on your buckle?"
We start jawing. I insist he refer
to my air-mattress as Alice. I tell

him, "She's all yours, she's my sister."
He says, "Ah so, of course, we're all one clan;
we're all grunts, and grunts are brothers."

"And thank you, brother dude," he continues,
"for your Alice, though here
in Wonderland, we call her a mattress."

HAMBURGER HILL DONG THIS

We've one foot on the freedom plane:
back to hoops, Dodge Chargers, football,
round-eyed nooky, moms, and ice cream.

But, first, we got to roll
the dice again up Sisyphus
Hill 937. And what a hill,

more like a green pinata stuffed
with body bags; whack it and here's
Nguyen measuring your cuffs.

And each flag handed to a dead GI's mother,
to cover her son smiling on the wall,
will hang like a tail pinned on the donkey.

A shame to get nailed to the wall
when Nixon says we've won it all: Blindman's
Bluff, hill 937, Hamburger Hill.

Since Adam was an igmo, Nguyen
has called this sore-tailed hump
not 937, but Dong Ap Bia. After eleven

days of American banzai assaults,
it's ours, Graffiti Hill, gothic
curlicues of spilled guts.

We leave fast, KIA vanity plates.
But in a month the hill's called Dong
Ap Bia, again, and Nguyen is right

back, king of the mountain,
playing Russian
Roulette, again, with anyone.

PEACE BARBIE

Lt. Ky's consort
can now blink eyes as round
as Oreo cookies,

and show lipstick Revlon Maidenhead Red,
and breasts a go go Maidenform,
and Booty Bucket by Girdle L. A.

She's hip hurrah American,
Zippo for peace and let's be rich,
highheeled Statue of Liberty.

KENT STATE CAMBODIA, DEAR MOM

We rolled Cambodia, found Nguyens
in swimming pools,
some skiing rice mountains,

puffing Luckies, playing ping pong,
and barbecuing pork
and holding hands. But when

the smoke unraveled and the world
looked up, we'd clanked slam into Kent
State. Shit, mom, we put four scholars

under headstones. A lick on them,
true, but it brought us four stepping
stones closer home, eh mom?

OO

First time I eyed her at
the club, she washed dishes—Olive
Oyl lean, but no make-up,

her long stick-neck a branch for two
Siberian almond eyes. I
didn't catch her name. She moved too

much like a ghost, like my
dear mother dear,
stepped out of the Fog Dynasty.

Mother was a heroic dishwasher,
suds tossed up rainbow trellises.
Back at the club a month later,

I found my once-dishwasher was, now, Miss
OO, her *nom de whore*—now a crotch storm-
trooper, advertising please do me please:

purple mini-skirt, red bra, and
yellow fishnets, lipstick
like she'd eaten a cherry bomb.

Now, my OO's no longer quite
the olive to take home to mom's
Four-Square Baptist meatloaf.

O's smile has the charm of a coin
return. But, now, at least,
she has a reason d'être, wants

a little white house in Dalat,
here in the Dynasty
of Suck, and she the First Lady.

THE EYE OF APRIL MAN

The guy who's lost his left
eye blinks the right one twice
as much to help the left catch up.

He winks that weeper like
a robot stud
let loose at a nudist picnic.

Let's give the dude
a medal or
a gold monocle made

in Hollywood. He's our
Romeo, winking for us all,
seducing the future.

THE MOHAWKS MOON SOME MOTHER'S SON

The lieutenant sports a Mohawk
haircut. The black
streak doubles as his racing stripe.

His troops wear this speedy braincap
as well. They're the Mohawk Moonsters.
When they zap a Nguyen, they don't cut

his ears off for a necklace or
stuff his weenie
into his rice hole. The Moonsters

respect the Nguyens too much to do any
undertaker slapstick. They make dead Nguyens
honorary Mohawks, clippers handy,

and SNICK SNICK Nguyen goes Indian
with the racing-stripe look.
He'll need this hot-rod trim,

in his race with
the sun, that chariot
unbeaten yet, pulled by western maggots.

And to give Nguyen some racing light,
the Moonsters drop their pants
and beam him their Indy 500 Moons.

DONUT DOLLY'S BOOBS

(July 1969)

We've won the war, now let's
shoot craps for Dolly Jill,
play games, cat call, wait on our jet.

Yes, we're the giant killers,
all of us Jacks still beating down
the beanstalk in our underwear.

And there's our Dolly in
a bikini—a fairytale of dummy flog,
our whole world on a string.

Strings everywhere. A man's a dog
leashed to his dong, and love his game.
A dog's a wolf leashed to his wag.

The only game here in this town,
now, is Cinderella,
as we wait for midnight in Nam

to bong. We're all glass eyed. We're all
watching this fairy tail shatter. In Nam
the only clock left is Jill's pendulums.

DIDDYBOPPING BUD POPPING

We're gone, leaving Saigon's Marvin
Arvns our junk, from gauze,
deep-sea ports, and Phantoms

to Budweiser and goofy golf courses...
leaving the tail between our legs—
all theirs, our whores their whores.

We keep only our flag,
our colorful magic carpet,
the cape in which we'll blast

off back to Chevy dice. We keep
our old Glory. Marvin
can have the pole. Sure, a pole with

no flag is an insult, like one
penis minus two balls. But sin
loi, Marvin, this is your Dear John,

the cards showed goodbye before Nguyen even
dealt them. Don't weep. We're leaving you the deck,
a better deck, too, only the jokers missing.

PRESIDENT NIXON SUCKY DOG

He's here in Nam prancing
in the Dog & Pony Show. It's
world-wide via television.

He's schmoozing with the troops.
No tie, short sleeves, his smile
a chrome banana he can't quite

swallow—
our Dick, our man,
our swell,

not the panty-laced rangatang
cartoonists sketch. He's got a helmet on.
The GIs have their headgear on,

all shiny green, the shitbird poems
scrubbed off. But they have shaved
the tricky Dick a message in

their hair, twelve of them have,
hair word under each helmet: DICK CAN SUCK
MY DICK ON WORLD TV IF I CAN WAVE.

These troops with their secret
hair telegram could be ambassadors
and wing the world for peace;

these crafty numbnut Kissingers
could glad-hand laughs and leave
secret notes between gunslingers.

These troops—they prove to Dick
the world is his oyster. But heah
Tricky Dick, don't crack a helmet.

COCKTAILS CELEBRATING VIETNAMIZATION

Nuthouse on speed—our spies
funky chickening, twanged by four
Nehru-jacketed French Monkees...

Premier Thieu and Ambassador
Bunker schmooze around, their sherry
nectar d'chrome, smiles hard as car

bumpers. What wit, merry-
go-round smoothies
of canned laughter. Plenty

of peachy-skinned Mercedes Benz
women, with their Venus FT cleavage,
stiletto heels, viper nylons,

and slits clean up to their roulettes.
Throw sevens here or lose
it all like a head of cabbage.

We've cut our loss.
Saigon now wears the chef
hat and her turn to cook Nguyen's goose.

But, heah, failure civilizes.
Lose your head? Crack a beer
and rise with the bubbles.

Thieu and Bunker coo their
Drive Safelys, smiles
flash like electric chairs.

Don't bet on Thieu. He smiles
too hard, like one of those concrete
jockeys who's lost his ride.

WHITE HOUSE TOILET PAPER

White stripes for bandages,
red stripes for gashes, blue for balls...
to honor the White House

for the act of cornhole,
for the, to wit,
act of screwing ourselves

with one hand tied
and the greasy whereas
in Ho Chi's hand.

White bandages,
red stripes gashes,
blue balls for all.

NAD KNOCKER NIGHT OWL

On Lefty's rifle there's a voodoo-tube
called the Starlite Infra-red Night Sight Scope,
which gathers night into a green movie.

Comes Nguyen creeping up in the dark...
Lefty squints and nails him in his
green balls. Lefty shoots only for the crotch.

Means a couple of Nguyen's comrades
must stop flinging hate mail
and lug him to their gangrene catacomb,

there slap a diaper on him made
of spiderwebs. Shoot one
guy in the nuts, and you eliminate

three attackers, all of them deeply gone
into philosophy with this fact to ponder:
a nutless comrade can't go to heaven!

It's religion: balls are Nguyen's stars.
No Testes Constellation means no heaven, must
be homeless through the afterlife, wander

around on earth, another horny ghost
and no Nirvanaland.
The thought blows any comrade's roof.

A Nguyen can imagine
being a corpse,
swelling like a purple balloon.

But he can't go so far
as to see this life and the here
after without his pair.

FRAG, THE MIDNIGHT SNIFF

El Tee informs Private Buddha he will inspect
tunnels next week,
his turn to wear the pull-your-ass-out rope.

But Private Buddha has a thought:
"I'd be scared shitless...like a lightning bug
directing bat traffic.

I'd get reincarnated as bat dung."
So, Private Buddha sends the Lieutenant
a thought to file under his lungs,

delivers to the El Tee's tent
a tear-gas valentine,
gives the Lieutenant a quick sip

of eternity. There's nothing
like smoke from a midnight whiz-bloom
to clear an El Tee's mind.

He'll understand how he belongs
to Private Buddha: each the other's dog,
the leash between them pulls both ways.

THE FOREHEAD MAN

Pain wrinkles his forehead
into furrowed hieroglyphics—
like his broken wrist is Egypt

sending his forehead telegrams.
The wise men in the tent can't help
but glance his way for a star bulletin.

Now on his brow, chariot-track
furrows run east as fast as west,
as if the forehead man's forehead

is a postcard of disappearing tracks.
Now the furrows bunch upwards in
the middle like a clump of worms,

like a tire-tread has rubber-stamped
his face. Now it's creaseless
as the Syrian plain.

The tracks of men, the tracks
of worms...and somehwere the Assyrians...
postcards from Homer of Egypt.

Why does he keep sending?
Why aren't wise men wise anymore?
Why do they keep looking?

BEEHIVE CANNONBALL HEAVY BLUES

Each round contains 8,000 one-inch darts,
people shredders. We found a Nguyen
stuck to a tree, rifle pinned to his chest.

No arms, no legs, no head...disk of a man,
a patty melt, a simple chest,
the rifle pinned across his tits, a sign,

a DO NOT sign—a human circle with a slash
across it: DO NOT ATTACK THE AMERICANS,
YOU'LL GET CHEWED UP BY ONE-INCH METAL BEES.

The GI's thought the burger rotting on
the tree would show the Nguyens what to expect
if they tried to party with the Americans.

The Nguyen's attacked again the next
night, left more ragged men
and guns posted to the tree trunks,

signs that seemed left by Nguyen:
GI, DO NOT LEAVE YOUR BASE CAMP AND SWEET
GUN, THE JUNGLE BELONGS TO NGUYEN.

IT'S A PICNIC
OUT HERE. AND YOU
ARE OUR DESSERT.

NOISE TICK BLONG

Sunday—April 1972—
the Catholic church at An Loc. Nguyen
pokes his tank through

the wall. A handful of Christians
scream, pots crash—clank
hubbub, dust...Christ unbangs

off the wall and breaks the knick-knacks.
Noisy as Jimi Hendrix on organ. Nguyen revs
a jeep in the pulpit. Flames shoot

from the engine, a coop of doves
on fire. This Sunday noise totals
on time's alarm clock not one whole

tick of noise. This whole wrecking-ball
day adds up to only one tick in space.
Helps you imagine the Big Bang and all

that noise when planets, quarks,
and UFO hocus-pocus
slam-banged out of God's watch pocket.

Now, that was noise,
when God's Railroad Rolex
exploded into life's

runaway freight. The universe
loves noise. This little An
Loc semi-tick is how life keeps

itself on track, similar to (same-same)
the My Lai tock, the Dachau bong,
the A-bomb blang. All these small-time

whackety whacks are just the Big
Bang Freight tooting time, redballing
round the next bend and next.

MOUTH A GO-GO

This girl
herky-jerked half
circles

and tried side-straddle-hop dashes...
this young lady—a mad disco
chicken—flushed headless from her cage,

caught there between Hanoi's
tanks and Saigon's jets—the music
of clinky doom and swoosh...

epileptic genius,
this demoiselle, chasing a butterfly,
her mouth the net,

screaming soundlessly black and white,
her mouth a black light bulb,
Auschwitz voltage and black spotlight.

And what did Miss Ballet show us
and her side show? Something
that might not help us catch a bus:

to trust the body, not the brain—
when all else fails, follow your feet,
two roulette arrows can't go wrong.

PEACE TALKS PARIS CAFE KITCHEN

To talk trash of the South,
the North calls Southerners *bean sprouts*.
Why bitch when you can cuss?

The South cusses right back —
gonug jing wikh yon — the North,
zee hung nun non, is *raw spinach*.

Both sides call truce to cook
each other's Last Supper.
Nguyen and Nixon the chefs.

And Father Time pops in to stir
in more bean sprouts,
then more spinach, then more

of night, and more
of day. Until, Nixon agrees
salt is pepper.

CRAWDAD & THE SECRET PEACE TALKS

(January 1973)

In a fifties Paris suburb,
Saint-Nom-La-Bretache, there's a house
where a sidewalk winds from the curb.

Nguyen wears suit and wingtips,
he's FBI and London Fog. Black overcoats,
hush-hush confab, so no road blocks

to hurdle or TV handshakes.
But what did they teach you in spy
school about these curvy sidewalks?

Inside, they're making the peace toy,
the Nixon V. Mudbug,
its fingers flashing V for victory

stretched toward the sky
like twin pitchforks,
got that big wind-up smile.

NIXON CRAWFISHSAURUS.
The spring that makes
it crawl backwards,

while at the same time smile,
is that curvy sidewalk. Nguyen winds
it up tighter each night.

And every day Nixon
crawdads backwards faster,
eyes tighter, smile wider.

INVASION DAPPER CHIC

Nguyen's at the DMZ
hot-rodding Russian trucks,
Chinese mopeds, and stolen Jeeps—

a Sputnik gangbang, but
Nguyen's only revving for his race
to Saigon, the invasion blitz.

Saigon's troops, bunched-up at the Z
to crush the raid, read Jap comics
and preen in mirrored sunglasses.

Nguyen just might catch himself
reflected in them so
Indy 500 cool that he'll bypass

Saigon and drive straight to the Carson show,
give old Johnny a yuk,
har har with Ed, forget rape and blood baths.

No, here's Nguyen's churning south,
Elvis down there—sweat scarves,
duck tails, curled smirk, and what,

showboating malarial shakes
and judo-chopping soap bubbles.
Nguyen's thrown away the brakes.

He's racing full throttle,
gun oil on hair slicked back
and straddle a bullet.

CIGARETTE MOMENT

The missile whacked
the jet, the jet somersaulted
like a tossed cigarette.

Smoke rose for a 500-foot
headstone, a tall
gray exclamation mark.

Here Lies GI Fireball,
says smoke,
its grammar unimpeachable —

no parachute
floated down like
a question mark.

SOLITARY CONFINEMENT ANTI-MATTER

Taking a crap when you got gas helps pass
the time—Mr. Cheeks, you're a different you
when on the bucket blowing donkey jazz,

the pumpkin soup
to thank. And then
the pumpkin soup

headaches also help pass the time—
two drummers bang inside your skull,
Ringo and Mr. Watts, they thump

so long it's like they don't want to leave you
back in solitary alone, your shadow flat,
plain you and no more headache stereo.

Then, back to watching time, the one long TICK
for sun passing and one long TOCK for moon.
You can do this. You are the King

of Time, or Queen of Time, or Dunce
of Yore, may flip-flop time: let TICK be TOCK
and TOCK be TICK. Slight mousy change.

But as Professor Cheeks, now philosophy cat,
it helps you ask: How can
one pass the time, but can't pass it?

THE NOT MUCH WEASEL CURSE

The POW pilots walk out the Hanoi Hilton,
past Weasel, who has fattened them
up some—Weasel, the prison commandant.

No more blinking
Morse code—T O R T U R E—
when tap dancing

for Weasel's chickenshit cameras.
And goodbye to the ropes that twist
a guy till he warbles curses.

The curse on Weasel is
he's a sissy hen-house rodent
with no more eggs to suck.

The world should thank itself
chickenshit tossed
on the water comes home to roost.

But the world's also cursed
in that weasels
never know they're weasels.

THE BOXED AERIALIST COMPUTES

Everett Alvarez is the first
American to ditch
his jet over the North.

It swirls down like an asterisk —
the farmers pause,
don't often see American fine print,

nor know much about Santa Claus,
but there's St. Alvarez,
sliding down the sky like his parachute

is a chimney. Eight years to sweat
out a formula for four walls — compute
it again: eight corners equals a box.

When let go he's so gaunt
his looks like a hatchet,
or worse. A hatchet has an edge,

a bright smile scratched on it
by the grindstone, but Everett does
not smile — mouth pinched — his lips

a minus sign that computes this:
Yes, you can steal
time from Jack in the Box.

PLUS RICE AND MINUS RICE

I commended mirth.

The freed pilots fly from Gia Lam Airport.
Wide grins and shouts. So many teeth
blazing they might be a dental advertisement:

NEW & IMPROVED SNOWY COLGATE,
FLAVOR YOUR LONELY PUSS
WITH JUST A HINT OF WEDDING CAKE.

Men with missionary haircuts,
wearing Salvation Army shoes,
now cruising over toy whitecaps...

thumbs up, flashing various V's
for Victory, V's for cleavage,
V's for the wife's new blouse

buttoned to get unbuttoned, V's
for crayon-colored pantyhose that lie
on the floor like a scribbled V.

Some wives have already unswore their vows
and have flung back the rice. It makes the news:
RELEASED VIETNAM PILOT FACES EMPTY CUPBOARD.

Shot down in Nam, survives,
but home gets run over
by wedding train racing the aisle.

Could mean seven more years of bad luck or
the best roll of the punch
bowl ever. Seems he had forgotten her.

A spoiled marriage—that's only rice
under the bridge. Nam rice, love rice,
divorce rice—start to taste alike.

PROPOSAL FOR HUNCHBACK

(March 1975)

The big child with the baby on
his back calls for mama and papa-san.
The house crackling in flames.

The baby's swollen tongue
stays stuck out like a teddy bear's.
Both boys could be ho-bo-ing from Phnom Penh,

or Florence, or Buenos Aires,
Stalingrad, or Atlanta—all aboard
to when? Why not? and where?

Their shadow's a hunchback. There should
be a statue for these children. And what
would stand taller than their shadow?

The kids may change—brown, black,
red, yellow, white—the cities change,
but that piggybacking hunchback

of a shadow always remains,
is perfect for the job,
and there seem to be plenty around.

TRAFFIC JAM AND RAM IT WHANG

From the air the traffic jam looks
like a necklace twenty-miles long
of buffs and jeeps,

goat carts, busses, and bikes—and can
not move. The colors—pastel pinks
and blues, sound of strangling accordions.

This stoppage is due to two Saigon units
fighting—killing themselves—to determine
if tweedle-ding or tweedle-dong will strut

at the head of the line. Typical of Saigon,
shoots itself in the foot,
while Hanoi blasts away what's left standing.

Hanoi works with the mind of a surgeon
cutting out Saigon's cancer: take
more than you need, as does a hurricane.

Twenty-mile gut, where stop
hacking? The flesh
so soft, shrapnel so hot.

Don't let Dr. Hanoi suspect you got
Saigon heartburn. He'll jerk the flame
out   \of your mouth, will grab your tongue

and rip it out clean down to your scrotum.
He's that gung-ho. No more heartburn
for you. And all you asked for was a Tums.

BABEL

Southerners fleeing Hanoi's juggernaut
bug-jump westward, scramble
like roaches snowballing toward the coast,

and throw a yard sale as they go—Little
Richard, Bibles, and halter tops. And when
these freakouts—shedding life wholesale—

reach the coasts of Nha Trang, Phan Rang,
Hue, Phu Cat, Phan Thiet—
what then? Hook a right to Saigon.

Once there, what? Hit the brakes.
It's Babel standing in the clouds again,
a house of cards made from the hope

found in fortune
cookies, tea leaves, rabbit
feet, and wishbones,

and horoscopes...hope that
Hanoi won't whirl
the South in a blood soak.

They yell for Las Vegas at Las Neo Babel—
Oh God, Oh Shit, Oh Buddha Om, Oh Holy Shit—
but all deaf as unflushed toilets.

THE NUTRITIONAL HEED

Nguyen's killing even refugees,
he's like the wolf
trapped too long, mouth a blaze,

and gnawing off his foot.
But all wars are nutritional
problems. Check Nguyen's diet:

for two thousand years had to eat Chinese noodles,
for ten years ate American eagles,
five years Japan's raw fish, and the poodle...

those miniature white French
Fifi's, that's what crazed Nguyen, poodles—
one hundred years of pink

toenails
and black velvet
collars.

Nguyen went nuts having to stomach
topiary
that pees, white poodles groomed

to look like shrubbery.
Nguyen flipped! Their tails pom-pomed
into heads of lettuce.

THE BABY CRASH

The strangest love letter
from Saigon rushed out by Uncle
Sam is a jet loaded

with two-hundred orphan
babies, address:
Land of Milk & Honey.

Uncle Sam, over for the send-off, says,
"Oh World: Sorry about the mess
we made trying to blow Uncle Ho's nose.

If only goofy doofusness
were a Kleenex
and if regret were bleach."

The jet full of infants
is still over the rice paddies
when the wind sucks

the door off, and Air Stork loses
balance. The air declines
the USA's parcel of tiny souls,

and the whole valentine
tumbles into the mud,
swoosh—a nightmare champagne

cork popped for a victory parade—
AMERICA FINALLY CONQUERS PADDIES,
as if fifty thousand lost GIs and

these infants didn't push daisies.
Ambulances squeal to the wreck.
That's as close as America's GI's

get to a parade. The one piece
of confetti that floats
down is the door.

CUCKOO KNEW IT

The Saigon soldier dangles upside-down
in the barbed wire that crowns the US Embassy,
dances like a dead snake dropped in

a fire. He tripped trying to sneak
aboard an evacuation chopper.
Had on banana-peel sandals—one peel

bequeathed by Pierre, the other
a Chiquita from Uncle Sam.
Couldn't refuse super-power slippers.

While he shivers, the Embassy marines
bash all the spook baubles—
no piss detectors left for Nguyen

to sniff, no James Bond smiles
to stretch. The sledge-hammers tick faster, but
the Asian wiggling in the wire

slows down like any bird,
any cuckoo
his time sawn off the limb,

one who
a thousand times
squawked to

himself that it was only time,
just a matter of WHEN before
the USA diddies and I'm

left behind like bloody drawers
hung out to drip. Those times
he warned himself of the future,

his words were only thoughts, a cuckoo chime—
THEY'LL LEAVE, THEY'LL LEAVE—a dry theorem.
But now his words are feelings, poems:

GI GONE TO THE SKY, JACK. COME AND GONE,
JACKSON, HIS ASS FLOWN HOME. That's the tattoo
the barbs prick deeper every lunge.

FINE-PRINT HOLLYWOODS

One of the last Kilroys
to get zapped in
Nam had ordered sunshades...

to better view Saigon's gardens—
grass and lizards,
lizards washed-out popsicle green,

Zen-Nothing grass. His mom put cash
in his bank. The Army had lost
track of him, not been paid in months,

as if the Finance clerks could telescope
the future till its past,
and this guy's dead, why pay a corpse?

The specs arrive, the latest in eye dress,
the wire-frame granny shades that John Lennon
sleeps in so Yoko won't look like a ghost.

I tried them on and eyed the sun—
the yellow porcupine kids sketch,
the quills shooting out like a crown.

Close as I got to being Christ,
to seeing a lizard puff pink his throat
like a turn signal, then back up.

MISS OLE MISS

Time and chance happeneth to them all.

A Vietnamese beauty waits beneath
the stars and stripes still waving at
the U.S. Consulate. She's dressed

July the Fourth: red and white skirt,
blue heels, blue blouse—American
right down to the platinum-blonde wig.

Could be a Chi Omega candy-cane
searching the sky for Lieutenant
El Tee, who swore he would return

before Nguyen sailed in on his tank,
Nguyen on his Mayflower,
uprooting everything that reeks

American. But no El Tee chopper appears,
no clouds whisk into wedding cake.
Will Nguyen torture her? She sputters

like a wet firecracker. She twists
and pouts, a barber-pole with breasts.
This haircut action may insult

Nguyen, as he's a short snake, hairless
and low; when the booster's
in the barber chair, he blushes.

How get on Nguyen's good side? Commie hammers,
forge them from her stiletto heels?
Knit red flags from inflammable panties?

What use for a sickle? The El
Tee's hockey-stick trinket on her necklace?
Or bend and offer Nguyen some tail?

And that would require more than ice.
Nguyen spoilsport—she cock her leg up,
he'd want a mask to face the music.

GONG SHOW NGUYEN, April 1975

> Let us hear the conclusion of the whole matter: Fear God, and keep his commandments: for this is the whole duty of man.

After thirty years of fighting Saigon,
the Nguyens now stroll its streets,
Kung Fu Nguyens, Judo Wingnut Nguyens,

but mostly rube hayseeds, teen hicks
from Hanoi's HEE HAW, hillbillies
goggle-eyed at the American wealth —

a dozen pearl golfballs,
a dumpster of Mr. Coffees,
a Johnny Walker still,

it all now Nguyen's, who could care less
about Sputnik, too far
out. Nguyen wants a piece of STAR TREK

and Matt Dillon's GUNSMOKE, wants six-shooters
that hit deadeye and don't need reloading,
unlike squeezing the Sam missile trigger,

the Sam a one-poof Roman Candle. Imagine
Nguyen's love of democracy when he sees
General Electric's toaster—warm

bread tossed up in Nguyen's Old Spice face.
And behind Door #3, a tanning-booth pagoda.
Then pausing for the thirst that refreshes —

can't you see General Coca-Cola
offer Nguyen the real thing,
until Nguyen wants to buy the whole

company, and will soon with the millions
he'll win on THE GONG SHOW. How win it all?
By sitting there demonstrating patience.

And so...how win it all?
Just fail longer,
that's all, outfail.

D.C. BERRY (David Chapman Berry) is retired from the Center for Writers at the University of Southern Mississippi in Hattiesburg, Mississippi, where he was a professor of English for many years. He has been published in journals too numerous to list, and in several anthologies of Southern writing. He has received grants from the Mississippi Arts Commission and the Southern Federation of States Arts Agencies. His other books include *Divorce Boxing* (Eastern Washington University Press) and *Saigon Cemetery* (University of Georgia Press).

Black Lawrence Press

Contemporary Literature

Black River, New York
www.blacklawrencepress.com

Because there's no such thing as
TOO MANY BOOKS.

Request a catalogue...
Please fill out and send this form to:
Black Lawrence Press • P.O. Box 9 • Watertown, New York 13601 • USA

NAME: _____

ADDRESS: _____
_____
_____
_____

E-MAIL (optional): _____

Stock up and save...
Please return this coupon with your order form.

25% OFF
when you purchase
one book

40% OFF
when you purchase
two or more books

Or order online at www.blacklawrencepress.com